AN EXILE

MADISON JONES

AN EXILE

THE VIKING PRESS

New York

Published in 1967 by The Viking Press, Inc.
625 Madison Avenue, New York, N.Y. 10022

Published simultaneously in Canada by
The Macmillan Company of Canada Limited

Library of Congress catalog card number: 67-20292
Printed in U.S.A.

The text of this book first appeared in *The Sewanee Review*

Second printing October 1967

FOR ALLEN AND DENNY

AN EXILE

I

"**Y**OU'RE GOING DOWNHILL," she said with vehemence and, he knew, turned from the stove to face him. The sheriff blew on the steaming coffee in his cup.

"All right, Hazel," he said quietly, and was rewarded by the hush that followed his words. He used it to look out of the kitchen window, thinking that this was just such an April morning—shot with gold and vivid emerald-green—as he liked best to recall from his childhood. Something out there in the yard struck him. "Where's the honeysuckle?"

"Gone." Bacon in the skillet had started to sizzle. "I dug it up," she said with the same hostility. "I'm going to plant some flowers there."

The sheriff could see through the bare fence now and across the intervening yards to the white blocklike building that was the jail—his jail. "I wish you hadn't. It'd have bloomed in a couple of weeks. I like the smell, it takes me back." He realized, even before he heard her shift her stance for the execution, that he had stuck his neck out.

"You don't need anything to take you back, you need something to take you forward. You need some ambition, that's what you need."

"I've got some. I'm ambitious to catch robbers," he said, and blew into his cup. That appalling boredom was closing

[3]

around him again; it seemed to veil even the brightness outside.

She made an angry sound with the bacon in the skillet. "A man of your abilities. Everybody has always—"

"Have we got to go over this again?" he said, humped over his cup. How he hated those curlers, like electrodes in her hair.

"Yes we do. Everybody has always said you're one of the smartest men in this town. You could—"

"Sure I am. You ought to see me outwit those crooks."

"You could have been anything you wanted to. You still could, you're just barely forty-one. But not you." From the corner of his eye he saw her arm, only her brusque angular arm, seize a bowl from the cabinet shelf. "You're content to be a sheriff," she added with heavy irony. "Perfectly content."

He had a childish impulse to low like a contented cow. And there had been times recently, fits of desperation not much greater than this, when he had yielded to such impulses. Then had come the rage and the tears. There was that other side of her, so easily wounded. He would rather endure her railing.

"When did I say I was so contented?"

"You go right on the same, don't you?"

"Do you want me to quit?"

"When you've got another job waiting for you. We have to eat, you know. . . . There's that new chemical plant. I know you could get in high up, with your name."

"You eat fine," he said in an expiring voice. But really, he thought, glancing at her spare rigid figure, she did not look as if she did. What person fifteen years ago—fifteen?—would have believed that such a shape of rounded flesh was after all mounted on so harsh and angular a skeleton? Hips that might have been bulges of naked bone under the print house dress she wore; nothing at all behind that a man

could get his hands on. Falling to bone, he thought. He tried
a diversion he used sometimes. "Anyhow, Sibyl eats fine,
from the looks of her."

"She's just a little stout." Hazel set a bowl of grits on the
table in front of him. "She's a growing child."

"She eats like a growing elephant."

But this time his banter inspired only the anger she flashed
at him as she turned away. "You ought to take a good look at
yourself sometime."

"I try not to," he said, but in his mind's eye he did take a
look: he saw his big hulking body slouched over the coffee
cup, the gathering swell of fat around his middle, the little
dewlaps beginning to sag from a ruddy undershot jaw. His
bulging wrists and hands like hocks of beef, protruding from
khaki sleeves rolled halfway to his elbows, were matted with
twisted bristles of reddish hair. In truth he was no prize; she
had him there. Fat husband and his skinny wife: that was
the way it was.

She sat in front of him a plate with bacon and a mound of
pale scrambled eggs. For color, he thought, they just matched
the window curtains—a lifeless sick-ward yellow. And spot-
less, like everything else in this radiant kitchen, like in the
magazines. How well he liked to remember that long low
kitchen of his boyhood, with tubs and pots in the way and
peppers in clusters hanging from the rafters. Just then a
breeze, sweet with some bloom, riffled the curtains; he
breathed deep. Hazel sat down with a plate of toast in her
hand.

"Suppose you had married Fred Herron?" the sheriff said.

"I could have." She flipped a white doily open.

"There's a whole lot more of him than there is of me. I bet
he weighs three hundred."

"There's a lot more ambition in him than there is in you.
He's the best lawyer in this county."

What if she had married Herron? Would that have made any difference to himself? He said, "And I'm the best sheriff in this county."

"Because you're the only one."

"Well, I'm a good one, too." Something ought to be said in his defense. "And they all know it. I never have taken a bribe or gone easy on a big shot or any of that meanness Carter used to do. You notice nobody ran against me. Even Hunnicutt. He knew he never had a chance."

"All right," she said, eating briskly now, eyes on her plate. "So you'll go on being a sheriff all your life."

That was a long time, he thought. He drew a breath, then started eating into the mound of egg.

There had been this interval of silence, but she had been only gathering steam. Now she got off on his past and the way he never had stuck to anything. Real estate, Ford cars, boats, and motors: all of these were prospering now, in other hands than his. As he raised the fork to his mouth he noticed, with faint displeasure, a little dirt under the cuticle of his thumbnail. But no, her voice was saying, those things were not good enough for *him*. Of course not. *He* had to move on to something bigger. To sheriff, she said, as if the job were something unclean like bossing a numbers racket. Which was unfair, because he had kept it clean. At the very least he had tried to, and tried hard. But he only answered, correcting her, "Deputy first. Then sheriff," and turned his attention out the window in front of him.

After a little silence he was again conscious of her voice, and now, penetrating it, of the sharp birdlike quality that came whenever she fell into one of her extended railings. Somehow it was in his mind to say, "Nothing is your fault." He thought he had come very close to saying it when, suddenly, something else replaced it in his head: a long sleepy wailing sound from down the valley, over the lake. "Mmm, hear that train."

He had not meant to say it out loud; in the pause his voice had wrought, the train whistle sounded more clearly than before. He saw her mouth set in that tense familiar line and thought, fleetingly, that the furrow at each corner enclosed it like stern marks of parenthesis. In a tone shaped to cut she said, "There's the very thing for you. You could be a train engineer."

"I've thought about that," he said and started into his eggs again.

This time the silence lasted; their movements, the clicking of china, and several times the smart flap of a curtain in a sudden breeze were all the sounds in the room. He got up at last with a mumbled courtesy, then stopped to unroll and button his cuffs. Again he noticed the dirt under the cuticle of his nail.

"I won't be home to lunch. I might be late tonight too, I've got to go to Finch and Gatesboro both after court this morning." For a moment afterward he thought he was about to be spared, but he was wrong.

"When did you ever get home at a Christian hour?"

"You mean eleven o'clock Sunday morning?" he said with impatience and stepped out of the kitchen.

He turned down the hall to the bathroom and there washed his hands, rubbing the cuticle clean with the ball of his other thumb. In the hall again he took his hat off the rack. From here he could see at the top of the steps the half-open door of Sibyl's room and one post of the bed in which she lay asleep with an arm, probably, under her head and his wife's black hair fanned out on the pillow. Hazel never would, for any reason, wake her before seven-thirty, and he did not see her in the morning. He never saw her much any time. Putting the hat on, he started back through the kitchen toward the door.

"It's just I want my daughter to have things." Her voice, unexpected, was softened; but it was those two words, so apt to his own thoughts, that his mind recorded. "*My* daughter," she had said—as she always said. It was true, wasn't it?

"She's got things."

"You know what I mean . . . I mean—"

"I told you you could start taking her to the Presbyterian Church." Her head was bowed a little and he was looking down at the top of it where, among the curlers, two thin parting lines made a pale plus-mark in her dark hair. "It's all the same to me. I'd just as soon not go to the Presbyterian Church as not go to the Methodist."

"I was thinking of you," she said, her tone rising. "That you didn't want us to. Because your mother and father were such strong Methodists."

"They are dead." He turned and went out the door.

Where had he got this habit of using the kitchen door? And this habit too, which he was indulging now, of waiting until he got outside and here by the sidewalk under the mimosa tree before lighting up his cigar? As if the house were not his. Through the first cloud of smoke from his cigar he looked it over: a small squarish dull-red brick with front door enclosed in a tight little cubicle like lips pursed around it. For all his two-years' residence here and the fact that that window up on his right looked in on his sleeping daughter, it was not a very familiar face. More and more it got this way, he thought, that nothing had the imprint of himself. Not even his own office, adorned as it was with the blank ugly faces of criminals and Deputy Hunnicutt's calendar pictures. Was it only this scented and poignant spring morning which had so sharpened his consciousness of these things?

There was no one on the street just now, and he walked very slowly past the small unfenced yards and the pale mimosa and maple trees. He could see down ahead, like a specimen for his thoughts, the new stone courthouse with white dome shining, and beyond that the hard polished façade of buildings that walled the lower side of the square. All new faces; now there was not one left of the old buildings he had known when he used to ride up to town on the wagon with his father. And not stopped changing yet—new names going up and everywhere strangers with fast fingers and dollar marks in their eyes, and the factories coming in. How did you get to know a thing that never would be still? He had stopped walking. He took a drag on his cigar and started again.

The jail, a patrol car parked in front, was the second building from the corner of the square. A brief strip of side-walk between the lush fig bushes he had planted led to the office steps. Hunnicutt sat reared back in his swivel chair, his feet on the window ledge, perusing a magazine with pictures in lurid color. He showed no awareness that the sheriff had come in; he wet a knotty thumb in his mouth and turned the page with a ripping noise.

"Anything last night?" the sheriff said and sat down in the chair behind his desk.

"Nothing but Dobbs." Hunnicutt scratched the bulbous tip of his nose and went on reading; he would volunteer nothing.

The sheriff reached for the big ledger that lay open on the counter beside his desk. Glancing at the page he said, "What'd you want to book him for?"

"Being drunk."

"Hell, he's always drunk. How can you tell?"

"It ain't hard." Hunnicutt kept his eyes stubbornly to his magazine. "Go in there and take a sniff of him."

"Sure, I know. But why not just let him cool off in there? You didn't need to book him."

"I done my duty by the law." Then: "Like you say." His head jerked a little; it seemed as if for an instant he had meant to turn his bottle-green eyes on the sheriff and then had reconsidered. The sheriff knew how they would have looked, with little seeds of hatred glimmering in their depths.

"I hope he didn't 'resist arrest,' " the sheriff said, just underlining the phrase; and this did draw a swift oblique glance from Hunnicutt. It was precisely the glance that the sheriff had seen already in imagination.

"He couldn't of resisted nothing." Hunnicutt spoke as if he held his teeth clenched. In the same voice: "I done my duty by the law. Just like you say to," and with this small triumph he turned another page.

"That's fine," the sheriff said, thinking that those eyes and the mouth that drooped in sullen lines at the corners most unkindly told the story of Hunnicutt. As everybody's, as his own did? In his own pale eyes that every year sank deeper beneath the ridge of his brow, in the lines around his own mouth, what did people read? But surely a story different in kind from Hunnicutt's; at least, he thought, it was no tale of a soul all but extinguished by its own vulgar and brutal tastes. Knowing what Hunnicutt was, he never should have reappointed him—not even for the reason that both of them had been deputies under Carter and that he himself instead of his senior had stepped into Carter's place.

Suddenly standing up, Hunnicutt flipped the magazine onto the window ledge and stood peering at the nude on the calendar he had hung there. "Be getting on," he said and scratched his ribs through his flannel shirt. Without the badge and the conspicuous ivory-handled pistol on his hip he never could have convinced a soul of his authority.

"You got to testify this morning, too," the sheriff said.

Hunnicutt only said, "Umm," and let the screen door shut with a clap behind him. The sheriff laid his dead cigar on the holder of the ash tray.

Now, though still subdued, there was sound of motors and voices down on the square. But here, there came through the open windows just such a blossom-scented breeze as he had felt and seen in the curtains of his kitchen window this morning; it riffled papers on the counter and the desks across the room. Rays of the early sun tinted the mottled walls an almost luminous yellow and the flesh of the calendar nude shone with impossible luster. And there it was again, the wailing of a train from somewhere far down the lake. Then he was thinking of apple trees. There had been an enormous orchard behind the house, old trees with limbs that scarcely would bend under the weight of a child swinging. They would have been in bloom now, a harvest of white flakes like stars impossibly thick in a green, scented firmament over-head. Where each one was, later an apple would hang. And he would gather them, he and his father, with his sisters to help a little.

The sheriff did not at first recognize the sound that had entered his reverie. Then he did: the door to the jail behind him was open and Dobbs was loudly snoring in his cell. This quite dissipated the sheriff's mood. It seemed to be the reason that his eyes came to rest on the bulletin board where were posted, under captions reading "Wanted!" "Wanted!" "Wanted!" pictures of faces in front and profile view. He noticed how each of them, white and black, male and female, shared alike in their expression of all-effacing blankness—as if in every one the last spark of longing or even of hatred had been finally extinguished. He got up and went back into the jail.

Dobbs lay stretched out on the cot in his cell, thunderously snoring, one leg in a painful twist hanging over the edge. His shirt and trousers were clumsily patched rags; he had a many-days' growth of dirty gray beard and hair that lay like thatching on his brow. Hunnicutt was right in one way: you could smell it plainly enough. Then the sheriff saw the laceration on Dobbs's right cheekbone. There was no way to tell, though, whether it came by Hunnicutt's brutality or by a fall. After a long moment the sheriff said, "Dobbs."

The snoring faltered, stopped; one lid slowly lifted, and Dobbs appeared to look at him out of an eerie fish's eye. It was a strange feeling, like sudden irrational loss of a certainty, to stand there in that filmy gaze. After a second the eye closed as it had opened, the snoring resumed.

Poor old ruin, the sheriff thought. To his surprise he heard his voice saying it out loud.

The sheriff had got through with his business in Finch and Gatesboro much earlier than expected; by mid-afternoon he was halfway back to Warrington again. He was in no hurry now, for anything, and he drove slowly along the winding highway, climbing the wooded hills in their pale early green and falling away into hollows where spring air held the freshness of daybreak still. The last of the trees, the hickories, now had sprouted leaves as small and tender as wings of a moth. There was redbud blooming on the hillsides and in shady places patches of white windflower and wild violets.

Twelve miles from town he passed the fork where the old pike turned sharply left and dropped out of sight around the flank of a hill; in less than a mile it ran into the lake. Ran under the lake, in fact, and on down the valley past where his home had stood. It was strange to think of it running there yet, in an eerie crystal twilight, as if it now could serve the need of underwater travelers.

The sheriff had been paying no attention to the rather battered and anonymous car, with a man and woman in it, driving at about his speed just ahead of him. What attracted him, finally, was the driver's face; he realized that it, a boy's face, had several times wheeled around to glance backward over a shoulder at him. Then he saw that the car was speeding up, putting distance between them. He would not have thought much about this either—he made lots of people nervous this way on the road—except he noticed that the car, now well ahead, had begun to swerve uncertainly back and forth across the center line. When he saw it keep on and then, as the car gathered speed on a long downgrade, get worse, he pressed down hard on his own throttle. The driver ahead seemed to observe this at once: he grew wilder still; his car reeled dangerously onto the gravel shoulder under a bluff and back on the pavement again. The sheriff, gaining fast now, pushed his siren, but it did no good. He could see the woman's head in motion, saw her white arm flash; this made no difference either.

Abruptly, the car's speed was checked in a shrieking of tires on asphalt and a violent turn that sent it reeling onto a dirt side road. Not quite onto it: the car careened off into the thicket, crushing bushes and saplings in its path. It had already rolled to a halt at the foot of a big spreading oak tree when the sheriff's car came skidding past the turn-off. The sheriff saw, even before he reached a full stop, that the boy was out of the car and running away into the woods. The sheriff backed up precipitately and cut into the side road.

By then the boy had disappeared in the thicker woods

down the slope. But the woman, or girl maybe, was still in the car—she had not even opened the door—and the sheriff walked through the green buck-bushes around to the shaded clearing on her side.

"You're not hurt, are you?"

She did not answer; her pale rigid face—like a mythic face in stone or maybe ice—only glared straight ahead through the windshield. This lasted a single vivid moment. Then he saw, under the blue boy's sport shirt she wore, her full breast rise with the long breath she drew to say, "Naw. I ain't hurt."

"You're lucky."

She turned her face slowly up to him and, it seemed, by this movement unlocked the rigidity which had held her jaw and pressed her lips into that pale tight line. Instead of hard, her lips were rather full and slack now; nor was there any such rudeness about her jaw. If her cheek bones were a little bold and taut under the clear just-olive skin, they did not spoil an effect from which, now, he was reluctant to avert his gaze. When he had to, glancing down through the woods, saying, "He your brother?" he still held the image of wide-set eyes that were more gray than blue, that had a curious depth. And that bit of gay red ribbon above her ear: unless possibly her age, it suited nothing about her—neither the brown disheveled hair nor her skin nor the obscurity of her eyes; and yet as by an accident of design it could not have been more right.

"He ain't but a kid," she was saying. "He just got scared. Because you was the law right behind him like you was." Her eyes had a sudden difference, like a change of light that softened them back to blue.

"He looked like he was drunk, the way he drove."

"He wasn't, though. He wasn't a bit. He just got scared. *You* know—like a kid will."

"Anyway, he's made himself some trouble. What's his name?"

Somewhere down in the woods there was a lone bird singing, and this had nearly obscured the fact that she was taking a long time to answer. She said, "McCain. Tommy McCain." A second later she added, "Mine's Alma McCain."

Without his willing it his glance sought for her left hand. But the hand lay half concealed by a fold of her skirt on the seat next to her thigh. Besides that languorous bird song, there was now a faint, a specter-like fragrance from some bloom. Spills of sunlight through the pale oak leaves overhead trembled as a breeze passed by; one, in a tatter of golden-greenish light, lay upon the flesh of her arm that had come to rest in the open window. "Well, I'm not going to hunt him out of that thicket. Where does he live?"

"You ain't going to arrest him, are you?" Maybe she leaned a little toward the window, toward him. "Please don't arrest him. He ain't but just a boy and got real scared. He wasn't drunk or nothing. I'll see after him. Don't, please."

Maybe it was her plea and her little leaning toward him, or maybe just a change of the breeze. Fragrance from a bloom, indeed; he drew the air more slowly into his nostrils. What trick of sentiment could so have stupefied his imagination? He said abruptly, "Why did he get so scared?"

She blinked, that was all; and then her eyes, very deep, were empty of everything except the pleading. "Please don't. It'd be a shame, he's not but a boy. Please."

And this checked him—if only for a moment. Just for now he did not, as he intended to in the end, lean over and put his head through the back window. He only looked from where he stood and was conscious of her watching the movement of his eyes. There was nothing to see from here: only a piece of plow line and a man's hat on the ragged back seat. From here he could not know whether that seat was a dummy on top of something else. Except for the bird song there was silence, and no movement, no change anywhere. There was one change, he now noticed: where her arm had rested before in the open window there was only her tense brown hand gripping the edge. He thought she was about to speak. The air seemed taut with promise of her voice and his blood was drumming in his ears.

But she did not speak, and finally he said, "Look, I've got his name. If he ever gets in trouble again . . . You see to him."

She blinked again; only that.

"You better see to him," the sheriff said.

"I will. Don't you worry," she said and then took her hand from the window. With another of those changes, as if a deeper shade had fallen across her eyes, she added, "I'm obliged to you."

He deliberately looked away, at the bent saplings and brush the car had left in its wake, and said, "You can back out of here all right."

"You're Sheriff Tawes, ain't you?"

"Yes." He did not turn to her; he felt vaguely like a man caught just at the threshold of escape.

"We used to live down on Sandy too, before the lake. On up the creek from you. We was neighbors."

"Yes," he mumbled. "I remember." Then, almost gruffly, "You can drive, can't you?"

Her hand, that had appeared again, vanished from the window. She slid across the seat to the wheel and set the starter grinding. The engine, unmuffled, came in with a hollow roar; amid a slashing and clatter of brush on metal, the car lurched backward toward the road. He stood and watched her. She was out of the bushes now; another grinding of the starter and then she was inching past his own car parked in the way. He saw her face glance at him through the fringe of brush as she went past; and maybe that was her hand he saw flashing a vague good-by to him.

Even after the sound of the motor had died and he was left with only the bird song in his ears, he stayed there in the sun-flecked shade.

II
___

THERE WAS A signboard—some tiresome warning the
sheriff did not read—floating well below the surface.
He left it behind him as he sank head-first into the depths
beneath. Although the light had grown obscure now, as if
filtered through a massive crystal pane, he could still see.
And suddenly there it was taking shape in his eyes, the
house with its long ell, all intact, with even the lilac and
the honeysuckle in dim bloom along the fence. How still it
was. Nothing, not a leaf or stem of grass or tiniest current of
water, disturbed this dreadful immobility of things. But then,
in the orchard, in green shade from the leaves and budding
apples, a boy and two girls were making a wreath of daisies
and crimson clover. The girls were his sisters, all of a sudden
beautiful, like swelling fruit in its first blush of color. They
did not speak, their fingers kept twining as they worked;
and that rich scent of grass and flower might have been
distilled from their young bodies. It was just as if they, with
their haunches deep in the lush green, had root there like
the apple trees. Then they too had ceased to move. He
remembered in desperation that he must have breath, and
he vainly began to struggle toward the surface.

The sheriff woke up gasping for air, in a room featureless
with dim moonlight. Probably he had made a noise, for more

than once recently his wife had waked him from a dream
unlike this one only in extent and vividness. But this time she
had slept quite through it. In fact, across the room in deep
shadows that effaced even the silhouette of her, she might
have been nothing but a sound of disembodied breathing.
Listening to it he knew that he would not be able to go back
to sleep.

Besides, there was the letter. He must destroy it. He
should have done so this morning right after it came in the
mail to his office, rudely addressed in pencil, with the word
"Sheriff" minus an "f." Even before he touched it he had
known whose name would be signed there. It seemed, in
fact, that he had been expecting it this very Monday morning and that the distress, a sort of mingled guilt and longing
which had kept him restless the last three days, had been
but the anticipation of this. Not really, though, except in
retrospect. He remembered feeling at the time that his face
was flushing, and he had taken a sidelong glance at Hunnicutt. But there was never any telling whether Hunnicutt
with his magazine was looking at you or not. And probably
it was Mrs. Brill, the part-time secretary, who had put it,
with the other letters, on his desk.

What did it say, anyhow? Nothing, really; there was
nothing in those two sentences that could seriously compro-
mise him. He ran the words through his mind again, weigh-
ing, trying to see behind them. But he saw nothing with
clarity, not even the image of her face in the car window. In
fact, when he tried to picture her he could clearly see but a
single detail: the bit of gay red ribbon in her hair. He
felt a little muddled—maybe partly because of the dream—
and he began to feel that if he saw the letter again, saw her
handwriting, it might help.

He sat up stealthily and, reaching for his pants on the
chair, took his wallet and took the letter out. The bedsprings

cried as he got to his feet; pausing, he heard no answer from
the darkness across the room. There was faint moonlight
through the front hall window and in Sibyl's room across
from his. He paused again at the head of the steps. From
here he could see Sibyl's bed and see her face turned up
like a wan flower in deep twilight. He heard her breathing,
too, and thought how lonely was the sound that sleepers
made.

Holding the letter in light from the open refrigerator door
he again read, in her meandering hand:

Deer Sherif Tawes,
Thank you a hole lot for not aresting my little brother
because he is jest a kid that got scared and wont do it no
more, I will see to it. I wood like to come and thank you
in person if I can.

Your old nabor,
Alma McCain

"In person." These were the words that most bemused
him. Did she mean anything by that? Twice more he read
the letter through, pausing over the errors and then the salu-
tation, as if these might give him the insight he was seeking.
Or give him at least the image of her face. There were
smudges, finger marks, on the page and a tear in the edge
near one corner. He studied even these. But only the one
detail about her, the bit of ribbon in her hair, would clearly
come and stick in his memory.

Seated now in the coolness by the open kitchen window
he tried to reason his way out of this bemusement. After all,
there was a simple enough explanation. They—her family—
were moonshining and she was afraid he had suspected and
so she was using this feeble means, her gratitude, to try to
disarm him. Wasn't this plain enough? He was nearly certain
he had smelled whisky somewhere about the car, probably

in a tank built under the rear seat. And he had discovered in the office records the name Ezra (Flint) McCain, most likely one of her family, who had been convicted nine years ago for moonshining. So, what was there to bewilder him?

Except himself. Of course. For her small, tired, feminine trick was working, was it not? He knew he had no intention of pursuing the matter: here was the bewildering thing. He, the Honest Sheriff, who had taken such pride in his own straightness, who never had so much as bobbled, whose virtue the devious Hunnicutt was afraid even to tempt. And for nothing, for a half-literate backwoods floozy who maybe had twitched her tail at him. Had he not come across many a better thing for the taking? Yet here he sat.

Well, so he did, so what? He looked out on the black moon-distorted shrubbery and then across the intervening yards to where, against the glow from lights on the square beyond, stood the jail in blocklike silhouette. What if they did run their little one-pot still and squeeze out their meager existence on the other side of the law? Whose law? Probably those McCains had been making whisky before there ever was any law about it. Then suddenly there was a law, with sheriffs and revenue agents behind it, something not any part of the McCains, something merely to be evaded. And he, the Honest Sheriff, executor of a law he did not make or assent to or care about any more than the McCains did, was here to see that they did not evade it.

Did not evade it. The sheriff's mind flashed suddenly back to the hour after supper that night, to the voice of Mr. Canning in mid-utterance:

"—that your husband is the first really honest sheriff they can remember here." He was the new Presbyterian preacher, and the unexpectedness of his visit had quite defeated the sheriff's ingenuity for escape. "Everyone tells me that."

Mr. Canning had said it, without even a glance at the sheriff, to Hazel, who was beside him on the sofa and who, at this remark, smiled fondly into empty space. She had gone, after all, to the Presbyterian Church the day before, and here the new preacher had popped right in behind her.

"Hank is an honest man," she said modestly, still into space.

"You're gol-dern right I am."

Hazel threw him a look, but Mr. Canning grinned in appreciation of his humor. The grin was maybe not entirely appreciative. Aside from showing rather too many teeth, it revealed a certain nervous muscularity in the sallow, still youthful face. There was something more to this one than pious good fellowship, some quality that the sheriff felt would please him even less. Probably it was this feeling that had caused him, after a moment, really to begin making his "bad impression" by plucking a cigar from his shirt pocket and vigorously biting off the tip.

"Hank." His wife's angry grimace quickly disguised itself in one of long-suffering.

"It's perfectly all right," Mr. Canning said. "I smoke, myself."

"You want a cigar?" The sheriff looked squarely at him.

Mr. Canning looked squarely back and said, "No, thanks. I've had my quota for today."

Here was another mark against him—this quota business. In fairness, though, in the circumstances, there was nothing the man could have said—except good-by—that would have suited the sheriff. And the influence of this small orderly living room, where he never came, did not help any. He hated this frail chair—not made for sprawling—in which he sat a little sprawled, the coffee table with its carved lace work, and all the fragile bric-a-brac that would fall to powder if he were to stamp his foot. Intending to make an effort, the sheriff straightened himself in the chair. But all he could think of to say, harking back to the minute before, was "Honesty is the best policy." Once it was out it sounded even more stupid than it did facetious.

"Hank means what we were talking about a minute ago," Hazel said apologetically.

Mr. Canning had not blinked. He decided, charitably, to take the remark as serious, and said, "Well, it's certainly good policy to have honest officials. It's hard to respect the laws when we can't respect the men who enforce them. . . . And make them, I might add."

Hazel nodded soberly. The sheriff rolled the cigar between his teeth, lit it finally, and without looking at her dropped his match into a crystal vase on the table beside him. "They're making them, for a fact. They got one for everything, now."

"Yes. We do have a lot of laws we didn't have before. But times have changed, of course. We need them now."

The sheriff blew a dense cloud of smoke. Mr. Canning waited for a reply. At length he appeared to take the sheriff's indifference for a challenge and, in a voice that assumed a hint of the professional tone, said, "I expect we all remember how it used to be. In those small communities most things were pretty well defined. Attitudes and behavior, I mean. They were simply inherited, so things were settled. We don't have that any more."

"Yes. Of course," Hazel said.

The sheriff smoked. He thought it might be amusing to ask Mr. Canning to pray with them over the matter.

"Sometimes we don't like it, we feel hostile," Mr Canning went on. "We shouldn't, though. It's really an opportunity for much greater freedom. Because now, with the wider knowledge we have, we can make laws that are a great deal more realistic. Men can't respect unreasonable laws."

"Yeah," the sheriff said and, in the pause that followed, saw Hazel gazing at him with suspicion. He dragged at his cigar. "You mean like in the Bible."

Mr. Canning's thin mouth just perceptibly hardened. "No. Those are not unreasonable. It's our reading of them that's been unreasonable."

"Well. Maybe so," the sheriff said, and smoked. "Sometimes I wish I was a little more reasonable, though. It might help, sometimes."

"Of course. We all do."

"It'd be a help to *know* all the reasonable folks are being reasonable about what the laws ought to be."

"You can only hope for that," Mr. Canning said with evident coolness. "There are some things you simply have to accept on faith."

"That's what my daddy used to tell me," the sheriff said. "He was strong on faith too."

Mr. Canning crossed his legs. It was his first obvious movement, a clear show of impatience, and the new position exposed a black-sheathed ankle as thin as a bird's. With something suspiciously like sarcasm he said, "And of course you have your voice, your vote."

"Yeah. That's the truth." Meditatively he added, "And I vote every time."

Then he saw the glare that Hazel had fixed on him, and he was quite surprised at the calm voice in which she said, "Hank, you know perfectly well Mr. Canning knows far more about these things than you do."

"I hope so. He'd be talking through his hat if he didn't," the sheriff said, and set about completing his "bad impression" by grinding out his cigar in the crystal vase.

But it was his crack about the hat, the sheriff reflected, that had been his great mistake. Through the brief remain-

der of Canning's visit he had sat there regretting it, antici-
pating the issue to come. And it came almost exactly as he
had foreseen.

"You were *bound* to know what a bad impression you
were making. You did it on purpose," she said to him with
real vehemence. He had turned his gaze aside. He hated to
see her face like this—twisted, almost ugly—and hear that
shrill quality in her voice. It made him feel guilty.

"I'm sorry," he quietly said.

"You're *not* sorry. At least for my sake you might have
tried to be nice. At least you might have kept quiet."

"Does he have to be such a pompous—" He checked his
tongue. "I'm sorry. I really am."

At this, with no other word, she turned and stalked away
up the stairs to her room.

Since then the silence had lasted. And here he sat with
the letter, the token that the Honest Sheriff was acting like a
downright Dishonest Sheriff. Or not acting: it was a "sin of
omission," in the term he remembered from his boyhood—he
supposed they still said that. It was a negative sin, which
meant a nothing, an emptiness, and so was as bad as any
act. "He is a nobody," the sheriff's father used to say in con-
demnation, meaning only about that person that he had no
moral character. What, then, except nothing, could be
expected of that person?

The sheriff thought about his father, tall and gaunt and
sternly righteous and simple to a fault. Foolishly simple, in
everything.

> I eat molasses on my peas;
> I've done it all my life.
> It doesn't make them any better,
> But it keeps them on my knife.

It was a specimen of his father's humor that the sheriff always remembered with particular affection. How it would shock the old man if now he could know about his son.

The sheriff thought once more of destroying the letter, but he did nothing. When at last he realized, because of the crumbled silhouettes of the shrubbery in the yard, that the moon had set, he left his place by the kitchen window and crept back up to his bedroom. Groping but almost soundless he took the wallet from his pants and fitted the letter in. There was silence in the room; there was not even the sound of his wife's breathing.

"What is the matter with you?"

The stillness should have prepared him; instead he felt the shock of one caught, exposed in his most shameful moment to peering, censorious eyes. For one instant of desperation he fancied that this had not been her voice at all. There was no moonlight from the window now and he could not see anything over there in the dark. How, then, could she see him? He answered in his throat, "Nothing."

He waited. Stiffly, clutching the wallet, he sat down on the bed. Amid a creaking of springs, like tensions in his body, he lay down on his side with the wallet under him. Again he waited. Again came her disembodied voice.

"You're not the same person you used to be."

Used to be, he distantly thought. Suddenly he knew why had come that instant's illusion that this was not her voice which had spoken. It was the different, the gentle voice that used to be; and in the darkness over there, in a gown that only clouded the richness of tinted flesh and sculptured female curves, she lay gazing with languid and passionate eyes his way. This vision passed but he was left with the feeling that his wife was about to get up from her bed and come to his. Nothing came of it at last, not even another

word from her. He could find it in him to say only, in a
voice he had not meant to sound cold, "I'm sorry, Hazel."

Next morning he destroyed the letter, on sudden impulse
burned it in the flame of a match he had struck to light his
cigar. Standing as he was under the mimosa in plain view of
the front windows while the paper flared in his hand he
felt in the act a sort of ritual cleansing. Yet his satisfaction
barely survived his walk down the street to his office. Seated
heavily in his chair, gazing at the lean blond head of Deputy
Pollard across the room, he felt as if he had just come a
long journey on foot. The minutes that passed, which he
followed around the face of the wall clock, did not diminish
his heaviness. And certainly the hour he later spent testify-
ing in court did not, even though the resurgence of his
original disgust raised him out of his lethargy for the
time.

"Sheriff Tawes," Pitt, the district attorney, said, "would
you describe to the court your procedure—the whole thing,
from the beginning."

As the sheriff spoke, he looked not at Pitt but out over the
heads of spectators toward the blank white wall at the far end
of the courtroom. He told how complaints had come first from
parents, along with a few specimens of the stuff—specimens
from the bulk of obscene pictures and booklets lying now as
evidence in an open suitcase on the table. He explained, as
discreetly as possible, how he had sought out first one and
then another of the boys at the high school until all signs
pointed clearly to the two boys already named. It was boys
from just such respectable families that these people used
when they could, the sheriff explained, because such boys
were likely to be more careful, more secretive. He watched
the far wall and told how he had gone to work on the boys,

one at a time, and at last by pressure of threats and also sympathy had managed to extract their stories. He explained how the game had worked, with the boys getting ten per cent—plus the other payment.

"You are speaking of the woman, of course. Nellie Wendell."

"Yes," the sheriff murmured. She was there in the courtroom too, looking damp and glum and colorless without her make-up, without fresh dye on her streaked ashy hair. Beside her was the man himself, Pendleton, sitting erect and composed, his seedy-handsome face watching the sheriff with cavalier intentness. All in the line of business, his face seemed to say.

"She is a professional prostitute, isn't she?" Pitt said.

"Yes. She was convicted twice in Nashville."

There were whispers from the courtroom, a slight stirring, and Judge Payne grumbled a demand for silence.

"And she was part of the bait, of course. Maybe the biggest part, with fifteen-year-old boys," Pitt said.

"Yes," the sheriff said, still speaking so softly that he could see spectators cocking their ears to hear. "And she was security too. They figured the boys would be still more discreet because of their doings with her. This way their sense of shame could be made use of too."

"How many times did they have intercourse with her?"

For a moment the sheriff felt like refusing the question. Then he said very softly, "Four, as nearly as I can tell."

"Where did this take place?"

A great surge of disgust welled up in the sheriff. He was aware that his voice saying "In Pendleton's car" carried an ugly and unprofessional load of irony. More matter-of-factly he added, "A place just off the Old Bridge Pike. A mile from town. That was the regular meeting place."

"And you and Deputy Beatty were hidden there and actually witnessed the proceedings?"

A barely audible snicker came from one of the spectators. The sheriff said, "We witnessed the exchange of the money. And we saw Pendleton take a package of that material out of the car. That's all we actually witnessed."

"The boys, of course, knew you were there. What was the woman doing?" Pitt asked.

"Just standing around. She did finally get in the back seat of the car."

"For the purpose mentioned?"

"Yes. Undoubtedly. She gestured to the boys. That was when we moved in on them."

Another louder snicker sounded. The judge's gavel struck the bench and in an angry voice he proceeded to threaten the spectators. Suddenly the sheriff was conscious of the ugly grin abiding on Pendleton's lips, and he had an impulse to spring out of the witness chair and strike the seedy face, to keep striking until there was nothing left but a pulp of lacerated meat. Of course he did not move from the chair. In another few moments he was answering questions again, but with the difference that now not even his disgust was enough to make him forget how tired he felt. He left the courtroom with an urge to go and wash himself from crown to toe.

The sheriff was feeling no different when later, in the afternoon, he looked up from his desk at the pock-marked face of the man who had just now entered the office. The sheriff remembered him at once: it was Bascomb, the revenue agent from Nashville. Bascomb sat down cross-legged in the chair he had drawn closer to the sheriff's desk and, while he talked, twirled a silver key chain around and around his finger. The sheriff watched the chain. Listening, he thought with complacency of the letter burning in his hand, its ashes drifting away on the morning air. He found himself looking straight into Bascomb's somewhat garish eyes to say, "What makes you think it's Rhine County?"

"We're not saying it is, necessarily. Could be Finch or Sorrel, or a couple of others, maybe. We just think it's in this area somewhere."

"Umm," the sheriff mumbled and looked back at the still twirling chain. "That's all?"

"That's all. No other evidence." With a very slight private grin Bascomb added, "These people up here have got the habit, you know."

"Yeah. Some of them," the sheriff murmured.

Bascomb stopped twirling the chain, closed it in his palm. "We'll need a list of those that have. The ones you've caught —or even suspected—in the last few years. We want to start looking right away. Like I said, this could be a good deal of an operation."

"You want it now?" He looked at Bascomb's clenched hand. Not until now had he begun to feel a certain uneasiness.

"Needn't be right this minute. I'll be back in a day or two."

From across the room by the window, "I can give you every one of them out of my head right now," Hunnicutt said and laid his tattered magazine down open on the desk. With maybe just a glance of his bottle-green eyes at the sheriff he added, "I been in this office ten year. And I got a memory like a elephant."

The sheriff, with that uneasiness gathering force in the back of his mind, regarded Hunnicutt, recorded his expression of stupid vanity. For the first time, he sensed in Hunnicutt some threat to himself.

"You just put them down while I call them off," Hunnicutt

said, locking his hands in back of his neck. "I don't need to look in no records."

"We needn't right now, I have to go," and Bascomb got up from his chair. "Be obliged if you'd get right to it, though," he said to the sheriff, ignoring Hunnicutt.

The sheriff nodded. Feeling that this was not enough, he had opened his mouth to speak when Hunnicutt said portentously, "Maybe you won't need no list. Just could be we'll have them caught before you get back."

The sheriff looked at him again. No, there was nothing behind that speech.

"Good," Bascomb said.

"I got a nose for that kind of thing," Hunnicutt said, and it was just as if he were presenting the red bulbous knob of it for Bascomb's inspection.

Bascomb faintly, privately, smirked.

"We'll have it ready," the sheriff said. Then: "And we'll start looking around ourselves."

After Bascomb had gone the sheriff sat pretending to concentrate on the report he had already finished entering in the ledger. He held the pen point just shy of the page, rolling the staff between his thumb and finger. In reality he was observing Hunnicutt, who sat bent over the desk, the magazine, with cheekbones propped on the heels of his hands. This was not Hunnicutt's reading posture; he was thinking—a process that required of him at least a forward tilt of the head. From out on the square came the rumble and grind of evening traffic; a distant whistle, quickly merging with a second whistle of deeper quality, signaled five o'clock. Hunnicutt was off duty now, but he did not stir, and slanting sunlight through the window distinguished the few black hairs on the bald crown of his head.

"You got any ideas?" the sheriff said, and found that he had but murmured.

Hunnicutt had heard him, though. He grunted some non-committal response.

The sheriff waited a minute. "Well, have you?"

"I was just studying."

"Studying what?" the sheriff pressed, in spite of his uneasiness. "Have you got somebody in mind?"

"Maybe."

"Well, who?" the sheriff said with a show of impatience.

Hunnicutt bounced a green glance off the sheriff and looked toward the door. "Thinking about that Leslie Peeks."

It was not much of a thought, the sheriff reflected. Peeks was small-time by nature, an incorrigible one-pot man with half a dozen convictions to prove it. Was it unlikely that Hunnicutt was lying, concealing some shrewder guess in hopes of getting the credit for himself? Could he be thinking of McCain? The sheriff said, "Maybe we better check on Peeks," then instantly felt ashamed of his deviousness. McCain's turn would have to come soon, anyhow. And, really, what was that to the sheriff? All the same, with eyes fastened on Hunnicutt's averted face, he added, "Anybody else?"

"Nope." A movement of lips, that was all.

The sheriff dropped his gaze to the page written in his awkward scrawl and slowly closed the ledger. He was saying now, "You can make up that list in the morning if you want.... Better check it against the records, though."

There came a just perceptible response. Hunnicutt straightened up and with decision shut his magazine and got to his feet. There was no response at all when the sheriff's voice followed him out the door with "I doubt it's in this county, though."

No sense in his saying that, the sheriff reflected afterward, for his words meant nothing. Either it was in this county or it was not; either it was or was not the McCains. Why should he think, when there were others he might as well suspect, that they were the ones whom Bascomb sought? Mainly, he supposed, because of a feeling he had come to have about the logic of a world whose pranking character it was to open doors and then slam them in your face. But if Bascomb's visit was another door slammed, then the sheriff's burning of the letter that morning had not really meant a thing. Then it was not the world; it was he who was tricking himself—still tricking himself. And in final proof of his self-deceit he tried again in vain to call up the image of her. A bit of ribbon, that was all. And tomorrow—or the next day, or some day soon—just as if in fact she never had existed for him, he would have to go out there as a sheriff and do his duty by the law.

Really there was no reason for his coming back to the office that night. There was no one in the jail right now, and if he were needed he could have been reached at home. His excuse to Hazel had been "I've got some paper work down there," and for once—no, it had not been so uncommon here of late—he had left silence behind him. Now he felt that he should do something in order to justify himself. His report was finished, closed up in the ledger. Still he sat down to it and under the shaded ceiling lamp, which he had pulled down to the level of his head, he went over it word by word. But this had been pointless; he shut the ledger and sat back in his chair. There was that list. He thought about this for a long time before, with a certain hesitancy of movement, he got up and went to the cabinet where the records were kept.

For maybe an hour, with ledgers scattered here and there in the pool of light on his desk top, he worked at the list of names. Finally, when he turned another stiff page, there it was: McCain, Ezra (Flint). He knew that all this time he had been waiting for it to appear and yet, now, it was like

an unfitting and quite solid obstacle to his proceedings—
words in a foreign language, say. He sat staring at the entry,
biting the shaft of his pen. It seemed that his eyes would
proceed no farther than the name and the date of arrest,
April 23, 1953. At length, like a man baffled, he laid down
the pen and tilted back the swivel chair until his head and
body were in the gloom.

There was now a breeze—at least he noticed it now—
through the windows and open door. It brought a faint teas-
ing fragrance of bloom he could not identify and made
inside the office stealthy rustlings. Only now and then were
there other sounds: a distant voice or a car going by with a
rushing noise or the thunder of a truck crossing down the
square. He could see outside the door one of his lush fig bushes,
see in the fusion of moon and street light the pale rippling of
leaves in the gusts of air. He thought it must be going to
shower by and by. He closed his eyes as if waiting for the
rain on his face. Later he heard a tapping of heels as someone went past on the sidewalk across the street, and finally
out of hearing.

There had not been any sound from there, he thought,
yet when he opened his eyes he was staring straight at the
doorway. Someone was out there, on the steps. He sat up.
When he did, radiance from the lamp obscured everything
beyond the ring of light, and suddenly he felt heartbeats in
his throat. It was then the knock came, softly. After some
two or three strokes of the pulse in his throat he said, "Come
in."

He could not, without leaning far back in his chair, clear
his eyes of the lamp's radiance. Yet he saw her take shape
in the doorway and enter as with a sudden and poignant gust
of fragrance from the night. Even before he could see details
of her person, the bit of ribbon seemed to burn like a tip of
flame in her hair.

III

"KEEP YOUR POLE still, honey," the sheriff said. "And watch your cork. There might be a big catfish down there sniffing your bait right now."

"Why doesn't he bite, then?" Sibyl said, again turning her round reluctant eyes to the cork that floated beneath the ledge in the placid water. That was her mother's note in her voice.

"He might any time. It takes a lot of patience to be a good fisherman. Sometimes it takes a whole hour before they start biting. Then all the sudden—" Again he grew conscious of his own voice, a cajoling voice that bumbled on in the noon stillness. Was its meaning so evident only to him? Hazel, at the other end of the ledge, in slacks and wide straw hat, sat as if entranced by the dazzling lights that played far out on the face of the lake. Yet for all her appearance he did not doubt she was listening. He hushed. For everything, all his cajolery and forced merriment, this outing itself, was too dismally transparent. Not that Hazel might have surmised the final cause behind it all: there were grounds enough in his old neglect of them. The really dismal part was that he again had tricked himself, had arranged this stunt in the idle belief that he really intended to mend what he had broken. And this despite that secretly all the

[35]

while he had cherished a different desire in his bowels. Despite, even, that he deliberately had not righted the list in which Hunnicutt—not, after all, so elephantine of memory —had omitted the name McCain. Alma McCain. Suddenly the memory of her body came like flesh itself touching against his own; he felt the tingling heat in his neck and jowls. The words he launched to cover his confusion said, "I used to fish all the time when I was a boy. I was a good fisherman. Not many people could catch them like I could."

The way Sibyl at once looked at him, with eyes a little narrowed in her round pink face, increased his confusion. She saw it. But what she said was, "That was an awful long time ago, wasn't it?"

It was not his confusion, then: what she saw, half believing, was himself in an altered perspective. She was looking to discover in him traces of that boy, that fisherman, whom the years had all but canceled by growth of brawn and hair and rank masculine odor. He said, "Oh, not so long as it seems to you. I didn't look much different from little Tom Stacey across the street. My hair was just as red as his. I was a country boy, though. You see all that water out there?"

Sibyl glanced out across the glittering lake.

"That wasn't there when I was a boy—before they built the big dam. All that was just a big valley, with farms. And a creek, Big Sandy Creek. That's where I used to fish. My home was just about a mile up the lake from here—that way." He pointed and she looked, but the thicketed bank of the cove stopped their view of the lake in that direction. Or was he right about the location from here? He thought of how the hills, even, cut off this way from the lowlands, were altered from his early memory of them; and he thought again how like a strange country all this had seemed to him when he came back from the army. In the eye of his memory, just where was this hollow at the head of which he was sitting?

"Is it still there?" she said.

"The house? Oh, no. They tore it down before the water rose. I wish I had a picture of it to show you. It was a big old clapboard house with—"

"Don't get your father started on that." Hazel interrupted in a voice hard and dry with finality. It produced not only a hush but a feeling of severance, like a shoot cleanly snipped off by shears. After a moment:

"I have to go to the bathroom," Sibyl announced, and the sheriff saw his wife get to her feet and take the child's hand and lead her away into the glade behind him. Pointlessly he called after them, "I'll watch your pole for you."

In a semicircle around the bright center of the cove were reflections of trees upside down in the water, and a wide-winged bird soared for a moment in the dense blue beneath. The stillness had closed behind him; the scent of water and pallid ferns and rushes along the bank seemed to be gathering freshness in his nostrils. Where was this place? The memory that came instead was of her flesh against his, lifting his pulse once more into his throat. He felt again the imprint of her lips and body upon his own and smelled the fragrance that had seemed to enter with her person. He knew—had known—well enough that she had come only for this, come to disarm him, in the certainty that she could. She had only to be a little slow about it, to sit there beside his desk in the chair he had offered her and repeat in her quiet country drawl the words that did not really veil her intention: "I'm awful obliged to you. Him just a boy and all, to get in trouble." Radiance from under the lampshade streamed on her full, now painted lips, on her neck, on her breast that swelled a blouse of some yellow stuff. But the face above her lips was in shadow, and he could barely distinguish her eyes. It was when he had leaned closer and first seen on his desk her hand with its bright down of hair—that was when he had reached out to touch her. As recklessly as any boy with his blood on fire. On a cot in a cell of the empty jail, as if all the people—even Hunnicutt—who might come seeking him were but so many improbable specters. And afterward, speechless beside her, he saw moonlight from the barred window falling in motes of silver upon her nakedness.

Yet even then he had not warned her about Bascomb. . . . What did this mean, though, when only the next morning he had let that list of Hunnicutt's stand as was? Unless he amended it: he could still manage that. But if the McCains were not the ones Bascomb was seeking . . . ? How, after all, did the sheriff *know* that they were? He needed to know. Even before his thoughts had finished taking shape he felt the quickened pace of his heartbeats.

"We had better go home now."

He started. Hazel was standing not very far behind him. He did not risk turning to face her, or even, for the moment, answering. He set about winding the line onto the pole he held.

"We'll go on to the car," Hazel said.

"I'm sorry we didn't catch any fish."

"Oh, that doesn't make any difference."

"I thought we would, though. I always used to; I never missed." He knew that he was prattling aimlessly. "I reckon my luck's just changed."

"Everything changes, you know," she said with a resignation that made him pause and listen to her footsteps as she withdrew. He turned his head in time to see her angular figure, with Sibyl in hand, vanishing up the slope among the trees.

It was mid-afternoon when he turned his car off the highway into a log road that was half overgrown with weeds and blackberry briars. After a hundred yards or so he parked it behind a screen of trees and picked his way back to the highway clearing. In bushes at the edge he listened for approaching cars, then hurriedly crossed the pavement. It was still a quarter of a mile to her turn-off, but the woods on this side of the highway were not so thick, and he covered the distance in a few minutes.

The dirt road, shaded by foliage overhead, was vaguely damp from recent showers. He noticed that now and again his feet left a print, and after this he walked in the middle, where tender grass was sprouting. When he stopped to listen he heard nothing but lonesome bird songs in the woods and, once, the far-off tattoo of a woodpecker. He thought he must have come something more than half a mile already.

Then, up ahead, as into a glowing bank of afternoon, the woods broke off. He stopped just short of where the trees ended and looked out at level fields overgrown with brush. Not all overgrown: there was a green, green pasture where a cow grazed and one area of dark new-plowed earth between him and the house. The house itself was a tall frame, streaked and unpainted gray in color, with a high turret rising from one corner. On top of the turret a weather vane sagged at a perilous angle, and farther down was a window with different-colored panes of glass—yellow and green and purple—still intact. At first the sheriff stood marveling at the house—as if it had simply been lifted whole from foreign ground and dropped, with not a little damage, into the middle of this treeless flat. Then he remembered. It was the old Gimble place, sadly run down, which he had seen once or twice in his childhood and until now had all but forgotten.

The same battered car was parked in the yard, but he saw no one about, and no movement but that of a few red chickens around the steps. Presently he left the road, keeping as he walked a dense margin of thicket between him and the open field. Before he stopped again he had reached the corner of the field, and from here he could see the collapsing back porch of the house and all three of the dilapidated outbuildings. Still there was no one. Lonesome bird songs filled the void, and over the house the pointed turret with leaning weather vane was like a sad monument to something.

He came on a path that entered the woods from the meadow. It was such a deep-worn path as cattle make, but there was only the one milk cow in sight and, looking, he could find no tracks in the earth. Farther on he did find, in a soggy place, something that might have been another kind of track—one made by a wheel. More, it looked as if someone had tried, though a little carelessly, to stamp it out. The path led on through a woods that grew thicker as he went and, at length, dim with the shade of many beech trees; then it began abruptly to descend. Just here he thought he saw the track again and he bent for a closer look. It was unmistakable—a wheelbarrow, probably. But what struck him now and made him suddenly stand up straight again was a feeling of being watched. Turning slowly he looked in every direction about the glade. There were only the gray beech trunks and columns of sunlight slanting down from the roof of foliage overhead. He started walking again, but he did not get rid of the feeling.

He smelled the lake. Down in a hollow now, walking beside a branch, he suddenly saw through trees ahead the glimmering of the water. He came out on a low shady bank and there was a boat pulled up and footprints, only footprints, in the mud. The boat was large, bigger than a skiff. Looking inside he saw nothing but oars and a bailing can. Could this be all the path was for? The lake in front of him was not wide; this was simply a long cove from it, an old creek bed. What creek? For an interval he stood trying to unearth the old geography in his head. Yes, it was Cane Creek, had to be, for that long jagged crest on the other side was Broken Back Ridge. Dancer's Mill. Yes. If water had not covered it, if it still stood, it should not be much farther up this cove. As he started walking up the bank he was dogged again by the feeling of eyes upon him.

The bank at length steepened into a rock bluff that he had to scramble up. From the top he could see that on ahead the water narrowed sharply, laying bare the crest of one old bank of the creek. A little farther on and he saw the mill, screened by trees and towering weeds, under a roof black-green with moss. In some way he was not quite prepared; he stood gazing down at it in a kind of mute astonishment.

He had to push through Johnson grass higher than his head, and he did not like this green blindness that closed him in on every side. When he stepped out of the grass he was close to the tall front of the mill, in the shade of an oak tree so dense that nothing grew in the brown earth beneath it. There was one sound only, a faint rushing of water from low down in the empty millrace. He saw that only fragments of the wooden dam survived, and he stood looking at these, listening to the water.

He had quite forgotten what he was doing here. He roused himself, sniffed at the moist air. Then he thought that maybe there was a scent. Looking about on the bare earth for tracks, he approached and climbed the rotting steps to the door. With pressure it came open on grinding hinges. The roof admitted streaks of sunlight into the dimness, and after a moment he could see the rusty corn grinder, one other machine, and ancient litter of cloth and metal scattered about. But the scent was clear now: this was the place. It would have to be downstairs.

The trap door, shut, was over beside the millrace, and he looked down where water swirled slowly at the bottom. There was no wall on the downstream side of the race; with the wheel gone, it would be no trouble to bring the boat inside and load or unload it from the floor below. That was it. He grasped the iron ring and, lifting the door, bent down into the mellow scent that rose from the gloom below.

There was need to look but a moment at all those drums and coils and those big silver boilers. How had they managed, secretly, to get it all here by water? The operation was every bit as large as Bascomb had imagined.... And now?

Something—it was like breath on the hackles of his neck—all at once intruded. It made him wheel as he stood up; he staggered and, for a second, teetered dangerously over the edge of the millrace. He stood looking squarely at the person facing him from just inside the open door.

Sunlight behind the figure a little dazzled his eyes, yet he instantly knew, in spite of her man's clothing, that it was she. She merely regarded him, hands hanging at her sides, in a manner that expressed nothing. It forced him to say at last, in a voice that he had to make aggressive, "This is what you were trying to protect, huh. By coming to me that way the other night."

She did not answer.

"It was just to hog-tie me, wasn't it? So I wouldn't come looking." But he heard in the tone of his voice now a difference not intended—a deflation that came of what he took for mockery in her face. This light—the brightness in the door and sun rays streaking the space between her and him—was confusing. Wasn't it merely his own false position that caused him to see her this way? He moved slowly across the floor and halted close in front of her. But the lidded and obscure gaze he met left him only more disarmed than before. He said, "Just to hog-tie me. It's such an old trick."

"I liked you too, though. I wouldn't of come, else," she said.

It was an obvious lie. Yet he found himself feebly casting about for something to uphold him. "How did you know I was here?"

"I followed you."

"I mean, how did you know I was around at all?"

"Oh, I seen you."

"From the house?"

"I wasn't in the house. I was out in the woods hunting ginseng and you went by on the path."

Even now he found himself conscious how her lips were shaped, how the bones of her cheeks were bold and taut, and missing the bit of ribbon that ought to be in her hair. "Didn't your brother or somebody see me and send you after me? They sent you to me the other night, didn't they?"

Her eyes seemed one moment gray, then blue, but they showed nothing. She said, "They never knowed a thing about it. They wouldn't of stood for that. I done it all on my own."

"And this too?" he said, and got no answer.

Was it likely? Why should he believe it? The force in him that already believed, that her words had inflamed again, was nothing but his blind desire. "Why should I—" What did it matter anyhow? He felt a compulsion to do something with his body and, turning, feeling her eyes, he paced across the floor, then stopped beside the rusty corn grinder. Oh, hadn't he already, in full knowledge, without a bobble, accepted what she had offered? Taken it as payment for what, in plain fact, he had already begun to do? Still she was watching him, passively. He blurted, "Look. Tell them to get this stuff out of here. And quick." He drew a breath. "The federal boys are looking hard for this; they know it's someplace around here. So get it out quick." He paused. "Tell them if they ever start up again I'll arrest them myself. Tell them that," he said finally.

"All right."

He walked back to where she was standing. He was conscious that she did not have to lift her eyes so very far to look squarely into his. But for all her height, her body and limbs were full, strong.

"I'll tell them" she said.

And then, he suddenly thought, they *would* know about her and him. But this thought happened as if at a certain mental distance; at the center of his consciousness was the triangle of bare flesh where the dingy man's shirt she wore stood open beneath her throat. In one brief spasm of violence he reached for her hand, got her wrist. It did not yield to him; she seemed only to inspect the throbbing hand that held her. Deliberately she freed her wrist and turned and walked through the sunlit doorway down the steps. He followed her.

She had stopped outside in the shade of the oak tree and he willed himself to say something cool, an apology, but he did not manage it. She said, "Not now."

"Why?"

"Somebody might come."

In spite of himself he mumbled, "We could go over there, in the woods."

"I better go on back. They'll get to wondering."

His suspicion appeared again, but only at the horizon of his mind. "When, then?"

He could see her profile now and he saw—what appeared hazily familiar—the line of her jaw unaccountably grow hard. She said, "I'll write to you."

"Couldn't you meet me someplace?"

"I better write. When I know I can come."

"That's risky. People see my letters."

"I'll get it to you some kind of way—secret," she said, and gave him a little unclear smile. "Tomorrow, maybe."

"But how? It's too risky."

"I'll strike on something; you'll see." Again the little smile as she started away, then checked herself to add, "You better go out up his hollow. You can get back to the road that way." Then, "It won't be long," and she left him.

"Alma," he called. At the far edge of the shade she stopped to look back, and whatever the words he might have been intending to say, he said now, "You never were married?"

There was just the shade of a pause. "I used to be. We busted up a long time ago. I taken my old name back." She walked away along the edge of the tall grass and quickly passed out of sight beyond it.

He did not leave at once. In fact he went and leaned tiredly against the big trunk of the oak tree. The gray, rotting, and desolate bulk of the mill brooded over a stillness in which the sound of rushing water was like a muted undertone. At length he found that by shutting his eyes he could restore everything to wholeness, to life—could hear the roar of water over the dam and down the race, and hear the thump of the turning wheel, and see in the open door old Lucius Dancer white from crown to toe with dust of meal. But when he opened his eyes again, there was the desolate fact, the very image of abandonment. Not quite abandoned, though, he remembered. In a way it was like a corpse that had been repossessed, whose empty bowels have become the host of a sinister, alien life.

The sheriff straightened up. Perhaps it was only this last thought that had renewed his feeling of eyes upon him. But it was powerful now and made him look hard at each one of the empty and the shuttered windows of the mill and into the thicket around him. He started walking up the hollow toward the highway.

IV

AFTER NEARLY A week the sheriff still had heard no word from her. Not only did he wait nervously for the mail; he found his gaze roaming to the most unlikely places—under bushes in the yard, into the gutter spout—as if he might find a letter there. Why had he ever acquiesced in so risky a plan? By force he kept the outward appearance of calm—he was good at that. What he could not control was the moods which displaced one another with such violence in his breast. Whenever he thought that now, after so long, there never would be any letter, then peace came on him like a balm. It was all over, this whole reckless crazy fit. He would just sit tight with his guilt, and hope for only a little luck, and hereafter keep his nose to the grindstone. But then would come a flat and desolate feeling, as if he faced an empty corridor with echoes and tumid light and no end to it. Until this too passed and, in its stead, there was the old heat in his bowels. All curves and lips and yielding flesh she would start up like a flare in his mind's eye. Old goat, he would murmur to himself. But for all his capacity to look on and grimace at his own brainless antics, this did not banish her. Nothing did entirely, not even sleep, for now she had got into his dreams.

Did he ever speak out in his sleep? Last night there had

been that vivid dream, the familiar one of himself sinking down, down, in dim crystal water. But this time at the bottom she was there, looking up, waiting with parted amorous lips. He thought that at the last he had called out to her and this was what had waked him. Could he have spoken her name aloud? No sound but breathing had issued from Hazel's bed across the room. And anyway, Hazel's silence toward him had been a growing thing of late; it needed no such dramatic explanation. His own self-conscious manner with her was explanation enough.

And yet . . . Once more the thought stopped him with a jolt. What if there had been after all a letter and it was she who had got it? She might have acted just this way. But was this more likely than that some other—Hunnicutt, say—had got it? Hunnicutt. He might have seen, have noticed, that first letter rudely addressed in pencil lying on the sheriff's desk. Suppose that somehow he had got his hands on this one. His hand, the left one, with fresh vivid scratches that the sheriff had seen only an hour ago. He looked across the office, but the magazine that Hunnicutt held partly concealed the hand. For certain they were brier scratches, though, and meant—what the sheriff had suspected already —that he was secretly poking about on his own. Where? But surely she would not have signed her name to a letter—or at least not her last name. Anyway, how could Hunnicutt make the connection? Unless the McCains got caught—then he could. What a feast for him. The sheriff got up and crossed over to the file cabinet near Hunnicutt's desk. Taking a folder at random from the drawer he quietly said, "Poking around by yourself can be dangerous. You know how some of these 'shiners are."

He did not turn to look at Hunnicutt, and there was no sound but the clicking of Mrs. Brill's typewriter over by the door. But he could imagine the look of malevolence, though blankly fastened on the page, in Hunnicutt's glass-green eyes. His own keen flash of hatred took him by surprise. Throttling his voice he added, "At least you ought to tell somebody where you're going."

"I ain't hid nothing. *Somebody* out of this office ought to keep on it."

The sheriff hesitated; he nearly turned his head for a glance at Hunnicutt. "If you've got a notion, tell me. I'll go with you, or send Pollard, like we've been doing." He paused again. "Where all have you been that I don't know about?"

The sheriff had to wait a long time and, suddenly, that flash of hatred surprised him once more. He had never felt it before with such intensity. At last:

"I ain't been no place but Corbin's, up to Warpath," Hunnicutt sullenly mumbled.

It may have been a lie, that this was all. Yet why should he lie? Why, unless he was onto something? But the sheriff could not press him further. Shutting the folder that had remained a blank for him he put it back in the drawer. He said finally, "Just tell me when you want to look into somebody," and got no answer but a grunt as he turned away toward his desk.

No, it was all too risky, too stupid in every way. Much more than likely, almost certainly, there had been no letter. Now, if one came, he would destroy it and just sit tight. He did not need even luck, did he, for what in the way of solid evidence could be brought against him? Only her word—if she should try that—against his own. With a sort of inner lunge he shut his mind down hard against the image of her. He thought of Hazel looking as when they had married, of their years together; he thought of Sibyl tottering at his side, holding tight to one of his giant fingers. Here, he reflected, was his only life.

And he persisted. When, after lunch, he suddenly encountered Bascomb on the courthouse walk, he experienced an almost joyful sense of release. No need, in the flush of those moments, to evade the garish eyes in the pock-marked face. "Well, we moved in on your county this morning," Bascomb said. "I don't guess your deputy's caught them yet?"

"Not yet," the sheriff said, checking an impulse to laugh. "But he's working around the clock."

"Doing a lot of thinking, I suppose."

"Oh, yes. That too."

Bascomb's small private smile appeared, and presently, on his finger, the key chain twirling. This gave the sheriff a sort of childish pleasure, even as he listened to Bascomb saying that they had had no luck so far in Finch and Sorrel Counties. They had hoped to catch another shipment, but hadn't; he guessed those folks were lying low, waiting for the wind to die down. When he stopped talking it seemed to be because of the checker game going on under the maple tree close by. He watched this for a minute or two before he started away down the walk and left the sheriff gazing after him with a feeling, somehow, of gratitude.

It was because, the sheriff thought, this small encounter had finally sealed his resolution. He felt as if he were quite safe now, on Bascomb's side, and able again to look without a flicker into any eye whatever. Even Hunnicutt's. (How stupid that feeling of hatred this morning, for such a wretched little man.) Even Hazel's eyes—almost.

He got a call an hour later. He did not have far to drive: the place was down on Mill Street, a street into which the business district had only recently expanded. There had been nothing but old L-shaped frame houses in the past; now the street was walled halfway down with shiny new fronts of stores. Just beyond the last of these the sheriff saw a crowd gathered on the sidewalk. There were trucks parked and a house in a state of partial demolition. As soon as he stopped he saw a pudgy burr-headed man in khaki and boots stalking toward him through a gap where the crowd had broken. The man quit biting his chapped underlip to say, "We got a goddamn maniac down here. Look at the old fool."

The sheriff could see nothing but workmen idly standing or sitting around amid rubble in the yard.

"Look the other side of the hedge, under the tree."

The sheriff saw a head of perfectly snow-white hair. It was old Mr. Linton; of course, that was his house next door. Through the scraggly privet the sheriff could see that Mr. Linton was seated on a stool, and that across his knees, at the ready, he held a double-barreled shotgun.

"What's he doing?" the sheriff said.

"I'll tell you what he's doing. You see that tree there?" It was a huge elm, umbrella-shaped, that spread far out over both yards and cast the shade on Mr. Linton's white head. A slack cable ran from a point high up the trunk to a winch on a parked truck. "We got to cut it down, it's in the way. And that old fool means to shoot the ass off anybody tries to."

The sheriff pondered a second. A hundred memories of that old man, his father's friend, came crowding back. "You're sure the tree's on this lot?"

"Course I am. Deed says so. Even he don't deny it."

"Well," the sheriff said, after a moment. "He won't shoot you."

"He won't, huh?" The man bit down sarcastically on his underlip. "Hell he won't. You walk over there to that tree and see if he won't." Someone in the crowd said something; another chuckled.

"Well," the sheriff said. "You people stay here, now."

He went down the walk along the high front of the hedge to the gate and pushed it open. Mr. Linton was sitting up

straight, facing the tree; his stalklike neck, rising from a
dingy collarless shirt, held his white head high, if not entirely
motionless. In fact there was a palsied movement that the
sheriff, approaching from a rear angle, never had seen in
him before. Maybe the old man was partly deaf too, now,
and this was why he had not looked around as the sheriff
came near. But he was not deaf; without turning he said,
"I seen you, friend; you stay right where you're at. Ain't
nobody going to creep up on me." That old voice, creaky
now.

"It's Hank Tawes, Mr. Linton."

Mr. Linton turned a filmy fallen-blue eye on him. "Hank,"
he said, like a name he had resurrected. Then, "Boy, they
mean to cut my elm tree down."

"Yes sir, I know."

"I been shading under this tree seventy-five year."

"I know. I remember this tree."

"They mean to cut it down. I ain't going to let them."

The sheriff heard rustling sounds; there were faces visible
through the front hedge and he motioned angrily with his
hand. Then: "I know how you feel, Mr. Linton. It stands on
that other lot, though. There's not any way we can stop
them."

Mr. Linton indicated, by lifting it a little, the long double-
hammered shotgun across his knees.

Gently the sheriff said, "You know you couldn't use that,
Mr. Linton. You know you couldn't shoot somebody for doing
what he's got to do."

Mr. Linton's hands made another, an almost imperceptible,
movement with the gun. The sheriff saw the Adam's apple
bob in his shrunken throat.

"Come on. Let's go in the house."

"I ain't going to let them," he said, but his voice betrayed
him.

"Come on. There's nothing we can do. Let's go in the house where we can't see it."

Slowly Mr. Linton raised his eyes. He was looking up into the tree, exposing to the sheriff a craggy and desolate profile, and he held this posture for a long time. When he looked at the sheriff his eyes were full of tears. In a weak throttled voice he said, "How come a man can't fight for a thing he's had a whole long lifetime?"

"I don't know. We don't know how to. It wouldn't do any good." He saw a single tear roll onto the old man's cheek. "Come on. Let's go in the house."

Mr. Linton stirred, that was all. But a moment later he raised the gun and set it butt down like a staff between his feet and haltingly stood up. He had already started walking when the sheriff, with a backward glance, saw again the faces in the hedge. He felt a violent gust of rage. Four quick strides brought him almost back to the hedge and, straight into their startled faces, he said in a harsh voice, "You sons of bitches clear out of here," and wheeled and hurried after the limping old man.

The shotgun, used for a cane, thumped on the wooden steps as they climbed, and on the floor of the porch. Inside, in the cool gloom of the living room, they stopped and stood with nothing to say. This front part of the house many years ago had been added on to an older two-room house of logs, and it seemed that from these came the air, the musty smell, of the whole. Stalwart chairs, familiar anonymous portraits, loomed out of the dimness. The sheriff cast about in his mind for words that would seem right. Then he gave it up and let the stillness reign.

But now there were voices from over next door, and now Mr. Linton moved. Carefully, as if it were as frail as himself, he placed the shotgun on pegs above the smutted mantel. He turned around, arms hanging limp from drooping shoulders, and looked at the open door behind the sheriff. "Shut that, boy," he said.

The sheriff closed it, further darkening the room, and the sound of voices was diminished. The old man gazed vacantly at the curtained door; his eyes seemed dry now and quite deep in his head. "I reckon I could get you a little drink. You're big enough."

The sheriff did not think this was really intended as humor, but he forced a small grin anyway and said, "I'm forty-one now, Mr. Linton."

Mr. Lonton looked at him as if at any other time he might have been surprised. "And sheriff too," he said. "Well. I reckon you won't mind about this little bit of lawbreaking."

His white head was vivid in the gloom as he moved, limping, through the wide doorway that led to the rear of the house. There came the noise of a truck engine starting up and a voice shouting something, and these drowned out the scuffing sounds of Mr. Linton's footsteps in the house. The sheriff started to pace. Now and then when he came to one of the big chairs he paused, and the portrait of an old face unknown to him yet familiar in character arrested him each time at the end of the room. He was looking at this again when Mr. Linton came back with a half-gallon jar and two cups in his hands. "It's a piece of lemon in the cup," he said, holding one out unsteadily to the sheriff.

It was clear, powerful stuff; the first sip made the sheriff shudder. He wondered a moment where it came from, and then forgot. The noise outside had stopped for the time and they sat in two big chairs, Mr. Linton dwarfed by his, and put and answered questions in subdued desultory voices. At length they quit talking altogether. He watched the palsied movements of the old man's head and, sipping from his cup, waiting, sat joined with him in a sort of alert and desolate communion.

Still it came as a shock, the sudden roar of the power saw, the scream when the blade took wood. Its shrillness seemed to bear upon a nerve at the base of the sheriff's skull; he noticed that even the old man's palsied head had become rigid. The noise receded, mounted again, achieved a still keener intolerable pitch. The sheriff shifted his eyes from Mr. Linton's face. The scream of the saw, interrupted by other sounds, continued for a while. But suddenly there was silence and then a shout. It seemed a long moment that followed. He felt it end in a jolt and seemed only afterward to hear the crash of the tree.

They did not speak. When finally the sheriff looked, Mr. Linton's head had started its movements again. Slowly the old man lifted the cup to his mouth and took a swallow and after a long time said, "It never took them but just a minute, did it?"

The sheriff had not had very much of the whisky, yet he felt a little unsteady, a little out of contact with things. He stood beside his car in the quiet street; the people, the workmen too, were gone. The tree lay disjointed, its limbs and soft green foliage in massive tangled heaps; and where it had stood the late sun shone on bare earth and on the yellow surface of the stump. He got into his car and drove away.

At length he found himself turning onto the Gatesboro road. He had to think of something, but there was a sort of void where thought should be and within it nothing would take shape except her image. He gave up trying to think; his vision narrowed down to the breadth of the center line on the pavement.

But now he had to think. He had turned off into the log road and stopped beyond the screen of brush and trees. But if he intended to march straight up to her door, what was the use in this? Of course he could not. He thought of the mill. Almost certainly she would not be there, though. But what if her family *was* at the house? He had the impression from somewhere that there was no other woman in the family, and so she might be there alone. He would go by way of the mill.

It was already dusky in the hollow he descended, and chill with the oncoming night. He tried to keep his footsteps quiet; the only other sound he heard was a dissonant squawking of crows from the sun-bright crest of the ridge up to his left. When he saw down ahead, where the trees ended, the sudden green palisade of grass he walked more slowly; then he saw the roof of the mill. Lest he make noise he circled around to a place where the grass thinnned out and he could plainly see one side of the building. There was only the sound of water in the race, and another, far off, of squawking crows. Cautiously he moved through the grass until he came up against the stone foundation.

He had already satisfied himself that no one was there when it occurred to him to wonder whether they had removed the still. There was a window through the top of the foundation, but it was boarded tight from inside. He made his way through grass to the corner and glanced at the empty clearing under the tree. When he stepped around the corner he looked up with a jolt into the hard face of a man standing in the door at the top of the steps.

Maybe the man had seen him already out of a window of the mill, for his face showed not the least surprise. Or was it because his face, with such a rude and massive structure of bone as strained the skin to cover it, was not capable of any expression? "Flint" McCain, the sheriff thought, recalling the name in the ledger. And Flint, as if to demonstrate its aptness, seemed prepared to stand there for good, with a thumb hooked in a strap of his overalls, and gaze blankly down at the sheriff.

"You're McCain, I take it?"

"Yeah," Flint said, with a sort of tentative inflection, as if there just might be some question. "That's me." His lisp, so curiously ill-suited to the looks of him, surprised the sheriff. It came of what Flint revealed by again opening his mouth, that apparently he had not a tooth in his head. "And you're Hank Tawes. I know you, badge or not. I've knowed you from a boy."

This, again so unexpected, for a moment disconcerted the sheriff. He required a second to adjust to his new impression of the man, so different from the first. He thought of Alma when first he had seen her through the window of the car, her blank and rigid look, like stone. And here, though rudely framed in the father's massive face, were the same bold cheekbones he pictured in hers. Into the pause came Flint's voice saying, "Yeah. I know you. I knowed your daddy, John Tawes. You used to come by my place once in a while, about a mile up Sandy from you."

"That right?" the sheriff mumbled, not remembering. Just then he saw that there was someone—no, two people—standing inside the door behind Flint. And maybe it was to draw his eyes away from them that Flint took this moment to come, lumbering, down the steps. If so, they paid no attention to the fact; the two of them, one very young and thin, moved out and stood side by side on the step he had just now vacated and gazed mutely down at the sheriff. Flint stood facing him, as tall as the sheriff—taller, had he not been a little stooped.

"Well," Flint said. Then, as if he had heard something, he glanced back over his shoulder. "Oh, them's my boys, Ed and Snake. Fine boys," he added.

The thin one, obviously Snake, acknowledged this only by a movement of lips not quite to be called a grin. He must have been around sixteen; and it was he, the sheriff assumed, who had been with Alma in the car that day. (Was there not, then, some truth in the things she had told him?) The other, much the older and heavier of the two, might as well have been deaf for all the response he gave. He stood just as his father had in those first moments of the encounter, looking like him, gazing as blankly as if the sheriff had been a post down there on the ground. And looking like Alma, the sheriff thought. The full sense of his own situation came over him suddenly. Flint was saying, "Yeah. I recollect just how you—"

"Have you got that still out of here?" the sheriff interrupted harshly.

"We're getting it out, Sheriff," Flint said without drawing a breath, even. "We done quit. We're going plumb out of business. Too risky nowadays."

It was far too slick, too easy, and this disconcerted the sheriff again. He could almost credit the old rascal with real, even sinister insight. It indicated that he himself would have to put on a much superior act. Or else mean what he said. "I want the whole outfit sunk in the lake. Everything. I'll give you just two more days to get it all out of there."

Flint blinked. It was hard to tell whether or not he was puzzled. The boys stood there on the top step like gazing animals.

"We'll try, Sheriff. It's a heap to do in the time, though. But we'll sure try." His hand came up and clawed among the gray bristles under his cheekbone.

"You better get started, then," the sheriff said. He hesitated. "And don't think I don't mean it. I reckon you know you haven't got anything on me. All I'd have to do is deny everything."

"Naw, naw, I know that, Sheriff. I know that. I never thought it. We get caught, that's our fault; ain't none of yours. I'm just obliged to you for letting us off like this. I mean, giving us time. Whatever reason you got?"

This last was not said pointedly or with any hint of a leer. The sheriff feared that it was he who had shown something: he knew his gaze had flinched. Yes, he would have to give her up. He was groping for words when Flint added suddenly, "I know you been courting of my daughter a little bit. But that ain't none of my business. She's a growed-up gal, husband gone. That's her business; I ain't got no say. I reckon she's your reason, but I ain't holding you no way on that. I ain't that kind of a fellow."

Of the questions that came to mind the sheriff could not shape one to utter. Wasn't this merely another piece of Flint's shrewdness? Certainly it had the effect of disarming the sheriff once again. On impulse he said, "Well, that's all over with now, anyway." But this, though he looked sharply, made no visible impression on Flint; and then be began to wish that he had not said it. Unless he meant it.

"Well now, that's every bit up to you," Flint said. "If that's so, it's your business."

The sheriff moved; he poked at the ground with his toe. A quick upward glance showed him the two wooden faces still gazing at him. It was only the light that was different, failing. He said, "Well." Suddenly he added, turning as he spoke, "Remember. Just two days," and walked away with studied deliberation along the edge of the grass thicket.

"Don't worry, Sheriff. We ain't forgetting," sounded behind him as he went.

He did not look back. At least he did not until he came out under the trees on the other side of the grass, and then he could see in the afterglow only the colorless roof of the mill. He walked rapidly for a minute or two, then stopped.

All over with, he had said to Flint. He never should have said that; she would be there now alone. He turned and looked behind him, back down where patches of daylight were still visible through the trees. There was no movement, no sound. Abruptly he started walking straight up the steep incline in the direction of her house.

The last dim blush of daylight made visible the turret of the house, and there were three lighted windows. He waited a moment to listen into the woods behind him, then started across the open pasture. As he walked he watched the windows, alight with a yellow glow he knew to come from a coal-oil lamp. He thought again that she might not be alone, but even this did not make him pause as he approached, turning the corner of the house. His feet resounded on the steps, on the porch. Through a cracked and dusty windowlight by the door he could see a lamp on a bare table and three cane-bottom chairs and a sofa with bulging springs exposed. He boldly knocked on the heavy panel.

The knock resounded inside the house. He did not see anyone through the glass and yet, with a click of the latch that startled him, here the door was opening. It was she, looking without the least surprise or emotion straight into his face. For an instant the image of Flint stood in his mind's eye, and then he could not think what to say to her. It was she who spoke.

"I'm glad you come."

Instead of an answer—he could find none—he stepped inside and watched her close the door, deliberately, as if she needed this interval. Her hair was combed as he had not seen it before, with a silky auburn sheen in the lamplight, and the ribbon was back in place above her ear. He saw then that her garment was not a dress; it was a robe, of some sheer stuff just lighter than her hair, that exposed the flesh below her neck and the deep cleft of her breast.

"Why didn't I hear from you?" he mumbled. "You see, I came anyway."

She looked squarely at him, her brow furrowed a little. "Didn't you get it?"

He felt his pulse recede. "You mean you did write?"

"Yeah. I put it on the seat of your car, in front of the courthouse. I waited till I seen you coming before I put it in there. . . . Yesterday, right after noon."

"You're sure it was my car?"

"It had 'Sheriff' wrote on it. And a star. It was in a envelope, with your name on it. It said 'come tonight.'"

Despite the fact that his gaze was fastened upon the cleft of her breast, he felt cold. "What else did it say? Was your name on it?" he abruptly added.

She thought a moment, looked away. He picked up the sound of a clock ticking in another room. She said, "Naw. It wasn't. I never said nothing about where to come, even."

"You shouldn't have left it there," he murmured and then was still. The clock's ticking grew clearly audible. He became conscious how desolate the room was, with few and decrepit furnishings, and cracked and broken plaster on bare walls and ceiling.

"Who could of got it?"

Quietly he said, "Hunnicutt. I think. I think he was using my car then."

"Who's Hunnicutt?"

"One of my deputies. A bad one to get hold of it, too. He'll do me in if he can." After a second his gaze came back to her face. It was in time to see her doing an odd little trick with her eyes—a sort of squint that appeared to contract each pupil to tiny points like diamonds catching the light. It was instantly gone, and now it seemed to have been merely a trick that the lamp had played.

"But he can't, though, can he? He don't know anything."

He thought to say, "I've got a wife and child," but did
not. For suddenly all that seemed once more far away and,
like the mounting fervor of his pulse, quite out of his control.
That soft flesh where her breast divided—he felt a tingling
dryness on his lips. Then he saw her blink, very slowly, as
to erase some meaning he might read in her eyes. This
teased him the more. In a rush of confusion he said, "I
guess it doesn't matter."

She looked away. With thoughtful steps she walked across
to the table and did something pointless to the lamp. He
stared at the shadowy nape of her neck, then down where
her hips swelled under the sheer robe. It seemed that the
very desolation of the room, even the distant ticking of the
clock, fed his desire; it ached in his throat. He moved suddenly. Before she could turn he had circled her body with
his arms, hands upon her breasts, and pressed his lips down
hard into the hollow of her neck. Abruptly his hands were
wrenched away; but otherwise she did not move. Holding
his hands at a little distance she stood submitting to his lips,
the pressure of his body.

This lasted but a moment. He felt one of her hands tighten
on his wrist and felt her murmur, "We can't down here."
She freed herself from his arms and, still holding him by one
wrist, led him across the room to steps that mounted into
darkness above. There were boards that cried under their
feet, a broad landing, dim shut doors around. But these
things circled his consciousness; at center was the pressure
of her hand and touches of her body when it brushed against
him. She opened a door, shut it quietly after them. There
was strange light in the room, and a glance showed him an
open door that led up into the turret. From there, through
the colored panes, a little starlight filtered down. He saw
her in this and, even as he reached out, saw the robe slip

from her shoulders and then the faint tinted luster of all her
naked body.

He had lain there with her face warm against his chest
and heard her murmur, "You ain't worrying about your
wife, are you? Ain't I just as good?" For answer he had
seized her once again. But now that moment was like only
the sharpest detail in a dream from which he was slowly
emerging, drifting upward toward the light. The strange,
tinted light. It was suddenly familiar: he was thinking of
the church where he used to go as a child, the stained-glass
window above the pew where he had always sat with his
family. Figured in the glass, in dull colors of blue and yellow
and red, was a picture of Jesus blessing the children; and
from that window there fell upon him just such a light as
this—a light that was the color of grace, that was God's
grace itself descending through the window upon them all.
It was grace, the preacher had said, that made sinless, sinful
man; and there he sat bathed in it. New-born in grace. Was
it not strange that now, with the sweat of his sin barely yet
dry upon him, he should feel as he had felt then?

He lifted himself onto his elbow and looked at the sleeping shape of her face in that light, at her hair loose on the
pillow and bare shoulder above the darker blanket. Her slow
sleeper's breath measured off the passing moments. He listened and watched, and felt no need of anything—no
urgency, no weight upon his mind or heart. Like new, he
thought: purged of the old body and the old mind. So this
was grace, and it was something he had found within himself, by merely choosing. How long since he had experienced
a feeling of release like this?

When at last he did get up from the bed—carefully, so as
not to disturb her—he did it with the sense of a choice that

had not been compelled. Chill air on his naked skin, making him shiver, did not affect his mood; it only made him hurry to dress himself. But when he had finished and had paused beside the bed to look at her a last time as she slept, he imagined that he was now conscious of something he had not felt before. It was enough to make him turn around and glance behind him at the shut door and then about the room. There was not much to see: vague chest of drawers, dim mirror, one chair, and the small open door where the tinted light filtered down from the turret. By now he had nearly dismissed the feeling, but still he walked across to the little door and peered up into the turret. There was nothing on the narrow staircase and, up above, only a greater density of light from the colored panes.

Her breathing went on unruffled when he whispered his good-by to her. He softly opened and shut her door behind him. In deep dusk at the head of the stairs he paused. It had occured to him that maybe the rest of them had come home, and this—a noise they had made—was what had distracted him. There was no sound now, however, from any source. Around him on the landing were shut doors, looking as if sealed in the gloom; down the stairwell in the lamplight half of the desolate living room was in view. Under his foot a stair step creaked, and then another, but he did not stop until he had walked out into the lighted room below.

He heard the clock ticking, very plain, louder than he remembered it. The door to his right stood open. It had not been open before, had it? He stared into the doorway, but he did not think he could see anything or hear anything except the measured ticking. Until suddenly he began to have the sensation of eyes in the darkness staring back into his own. It grew so strong that after a second he looked down, looked self-consciously at his watch without his mind's recording the hour. But whatever the time, it seemed excuse enough for his departure. He hung there a moment longer, however, held back by shame at the thought that he was fleeing. In fact he lifted his eyes in a last brief stare of defiance. Not until he was outside walking swiftly along the road did he begin to doubt that there had been anyone in that room.

V

THE SHERIFF'S FEELING of renewal did not pass off with a night's sleep. Rather it seemed to increase, feeding the boldness of his desire. In the course of the next few days he went twice to see her. For the first of these visits—since he had made no arrangement with her and still would not risk a note—he had simply screwed up his nerve and barged in, hoping. This time he had luck: she was there alone. She was alone the next time too, as she had said she would be, but he was nearly sure that this was not by any chance arrangement. He knew, in fact, without letting himself think much about it, that he was certainly participating in an arrangement which involved not only her and himself. He would somehow protect them, and they in return would wink at all his antics. He even knew, must have known, that they had no intention of getting out of business—not as long as they had him. He did not think about this either; he tried to think only about her and about the desire that he did not any longer even want to quench.

He had not become equally reckless otherwise, however. In fact, where Hunnicutt was concerned he grew increasingly wary. The sneaking wretch had tried to follow him night before last—proof enough that he had got the note. The sheriff, that time, had been on his way only to Buck's Crossing, so this had been to the good: he was forewarned now. What troubled him far more—if the two things could be kept separate in his mind—was Hunnicutt's diligence in the whisky matter. Although Hunnicutt was slyer than ever he still was not giving up. In proof of this the sheriff had surprised him, at night, turning through some of the old ledgers he had put out on the counter. He had not yet got to the one with McCain's name, and when, moments later, with a clumsy show of disdain he had put them back in the cabinet, the sheriff made his decision. He had thought of it before this, and hesitated. Now, when Hunnicutt had gone, he took out the ledger and with great care removed the page. He did not think it could be noticed. And if so, why should he be suspected?

But this did not relieve him for long. There were other things—accidents, people—that might easily strike a spark in Hunnicutt's memory. There was something that could be done, however. All day the sheriff turned the idea backward and forward in his mind. He could find no fault in it—unless it was that already he had removed that page from the ledger. That night when he visited Alma he explained his plan and instructed her in detail as to what precautions must be taken.

He was planning it for the next morning, and through the wakeful remainder of the night he thought of little else. At breakfast time he was still so intent upon it that he failed to notice not only his wife's silence but even her presence at the table. Or he did until suddenly:

"I'm going down to Gatesboro to stay with Sister."

This penetrated. In fact it set off a kind of shrill alarm in some neglected region of his mind. For the first time in many days he was flatly confronted with the seriousness—in truth, the folly—of his behavior. How much had she seen of it? And what had others seen? Mastering his feeling, he said, "When did this come up?"

"Last night. She called me up. You weren't here."

He fooled with his coffee cup and did not lift his head to ask, "How long are you going to stay?"

"Until she's better, anyhow."

"She's been this way a long time, you know."

"No, she's worse than she was," Hazel said in a voice that concluded things. Or almost concluded them: later she broke the silence to add, "Dora will come in the mornings. She'll fix your breakfast. You won't miss us much."

"Of course I will," he said uneasily. "What do you mean?"

She did not answer; she got up from the table with half-filled plate and cup in her hand.

"I'll miss you both," he said. At length, quite meaning it for the moment, he added, "I wish you wouldn't go."

But she did not answer. And even before she was ready to leave, his mood of alarm had receded again into that same neglected region of his mind.

Despite his impatience, contained with effort, he had to drive them to Gatesboro. He was thankful for the hard rain that obscured the windshield and drummed upon the roof, and for the humming and occasional phrases of tune-less song that came from Sibyl in the back seat: these helped to keep their feeble display of naturalness intact. Sometimes from the corner of his eye he would look at Hazel, intent on the road, with sharp-featured face and small pie-pan hat set precisely forward over her brow. He thought what a comfortable kind of noise was that railing which for him had been a fixture of her company. And each time he would wonder, with a new surge of that venom in his breast, whether it could be that Hunnicutt had found some way to tell her what he knew. But it was not likely; this between Hazel and himself was a growth which had not escaped even his inattentiveness. . . . Unless she read him deeper than he thought. He shut his mind on this.

In fact, he ended by shutting his mind on everything that might have pressed home the meaning of that trip. Except for one detail: this somehow had got inside and stuck. It was not Hazel's last glancing look at him as he stood in the hall with her and the haggard, bathrobed Ann, or the coolness of the cheek his lips had brushed. It was a glimpse he had got through the door of the living room: Sibyl already in the big rocking chair, feet swinging shy of the floor as she rocked, a look of pleased contentment on her face.

But even this, soon enough, got obscured behind the other matter—that of disarming Hunnicutt. On the drive back to Warrington he turned it over and over. He did not see why it should not go off smoothly: he need only keep his wits about him—and antagonize Hunnicutt a little.

And it did go off almost as he had planned, that same afternoon. He launched it in just the right tone of voice. Leaning far back in his swivel chair, hands clasped behind his neck, he said, "Hunnicutt, how's your memory for old moonshiners?"

Hunnicutt, from behind his magazine, gave him a suspicious glance.

"You sure you've remembered *all* of them?"

Hunnicutt looked at him now, with hostile eyes.

"You don't reckon you could have forgotten just *one?*"

"What you getting at?"

"I've been doing some poking around, myself. Looks mighty like you forgot one, anyhow. So maybe there are still some more."

"Who'd I forget?" Hunnicutt said.

"You ever hear the name McCain?" It had sounded natural, he thought; yet he felt a certain after-shock, as if he had just now committed a ruinous blunder. He found he was holding his breath. Hunnicutt's eyes had registered something. His voice, however, did not yield a thing.

"I done already thought of him. I been—"

"Why wasn't he on your list, then?"

This stumped him for a second; his underlip hung slack. It gave the sheriff a dim satisfaction.

"Maybe I didn't recollect him right off," Hunnicutt said defiantly. "But it wasn't long; I don't never forget one long. I'd of put him in there before now but I ain't seen that Bascomb fellow."

"You could have told me, couldn't you?" The sheriff let him fumble. In his own breast he felt again a response to the hatred growing in Hunnicutt's eyes. "Well, we better check on him. That list of yours hasn't turned up anything."

"Yeah, well, this'n ain't likely to neither," Hunnicutt shot back. "That's how come I wasn't in no bigger hurry about him."

This was just what the sheriff had wanted. To make it stronger he added, "Looks to me like just about as good a chance as the others. We might as well get out there and check."

Hunnicutt's skeptical sneer, now and then repeated as they drove out the highway in thin misting rain, was still a satisfaction to the sheriff. But now he put it out of mind: he had to start concentrating. As they drew near the turn-off he began to drive very slowly. "That ought to be it up ahead there—where the mailbox is."

"You're the one knows," Hunnicutt answered. He had his wide-brimmed Texas hat pushed far back on his head.

They had rolled to a stop. "We need somewhere to put the car out of sight." A moment later he pretended to notice the log road just behind them to their left. "That ought to do," he said, and backed up, then turned off into the overgrown road.

"Somebody been using it lately," Hunnicutt said as they came to a stop between clumps of green buck-bushes.

"Hunters, I reckon."

"What they hunt this time of the year?"

It was a small slip, not important. "Well, boys and girls, then," he said, getting out. But he had to be more careful; he must not give Hunnicutt occasion to pride himself on his alertness. He was glad to see that Hunnicutt made no effort to keep abreast but stayed a pace or two behind and followed him across the highway and into the dripping woods. Now and again as they went on, drops of water from a bush or a low-hanging branch showered down on them. Hunnicutt said, "Could have waited till it stopped raining, anyhow."

This was just the tone that the sheriff wanted to hear. "You got on a raincoat," was all he said.

They came out on the dirt road and, without a word, slogged through mud and puddles to where the woods ended and they could see the house. There was no one, no car in sight.

"Funny-looking house," Hunnicutt said. "Like it started out to be a church." Water dripped from the awning-like brim of his hat.

"That's the old Gimble house, I think," the sheriff said, looking at it through the mist of rain. Was she there now? In her room with the tinted light, in the bed where her naked body's aura was like midsummer heat? He mumbled, "I remember seeing it when I was a kid."

"We never had nothing like *that* down at Pelham," Hunnicutt said, as if the fact were something in which he took pride.

The sheriff led off to his left, through the woods on a gentle downgrade that he knew must end at last in a hollow. The fine rain continued to fall. Their feet made little noise in the wet leaves and the ferns as they descended or climbed another ridge or walked another hollow back to its head. On purpose the sheriff moved fast. Hunnicutt, still lagging, forced a pause now and then to wipe the sweat that rolled from under his Texas hat. At the crest of a ridge, panting, he said, "If it's big as that Bascomb says. . . goin' t' be *in* something, ain't it? How come them airplanes ain't spotted it?"

"Maybe," the sheriff said. "But they got ways of camouflaging them."

Several times they got a view of the lake, its slate-gray surface prickled by the rain, with pale mist that lay afloat in motionless threads and tatters. The sheriff led on with an energy that seemed but to gather impulse from his pounding heart and swelling lungs. It gave him a feeling of release, of exuberance even, to strain his body this way; especially when a backward glance showed him the laboring figure of Hunnicutt. "What the hell?" Hunnicutt would gasp. "What in hell's the hurry?"

"Come on. We haven't got all night."

But all the while the sheriff was calculating. When finally, circling, they came up on the east side of the pasture and the house, there remained not an hour of daylight. They stopped and stood there in the edge of the woods, panting.

"You ought to brought a gang," Hunnicutt said, "if you aimed on covering the whole country."

"We'll have this one off the list, anyhow," the sheriff said. After a moment, glancing at Hunnicutt, "How many more do you reckon you forgot?"

With a flash of green eyes, "I told you," Hunnicutt snapped. "I didn't forget this'n. But just a day or two— because of it not looking like much of a bet. We ain't found nothing, have we?"

"We're not through yet."

"All right. Let's get through."

Hunnicutt had already started to turn when something caught his eye. Looking, the sheriff saw that it was Alma approaching the pump in back of the house with a bucket in her hand. Why hadn't she stayed inside? Fortunately they were a good long distance from her and the air was misty with rain.

"Who's that?" Hunnicutt said.

"I don't know. A woman. Every house has got one."

"Young-looking," Hunnicutt said, squinting. "I ain't seen nobody else."

"They all work in town." Lest this seem too knowing, he added quickly, "I checked on them."

"Who's 'them'?"

"Father and a couple of boys."

"Well." Hunnicutt stared. Alma was working the pump now, her bare arm flashing pale in the grayness of the atmosphere. "Looks like the little lady's all by her lonesome in the daytime, don't it?" With a smirk: "We might ought to just drop in some morning and make a little company for her."

Rage flared in the sheriff's blood. Knowing that it must plainly show in his face, he turned his head away. But apparently Hunnicutt had noticed. He said, "But I reckon you're too pure of heart for such as that, ain't you?"

The sheriff stood staring blankly across the pasture. In a tight voice he said, "What do you mean?"

"Aw, just I know what kind of a pure-hearted fellow you are."

The sheriff choked back words that would have come, clamped his teeth together. Abruptly turning, "Come on; we haven't got all night," he said and started off through the woods.

He had not gone many steps when suddenly, through his rage, he heard in back of him, "Hey, you run right over this path here." He wheeled around, too late, then turned his silent curses against himself. For already Hunnicutt, like a hound on a hot track, was leading off swiftly down the path with a new-found air of authority. It was maybe a serious slip for the sheriff; there was nothing he could do now but follow, for Hunnicutt clearly meant to lead.

He led on rapidly, into thickening timber, through the dripping and shadowy grove of beech. "This path been used a heap," Hunnicutt said, without looking back, in his most portentous voice.

"Yeah," the sheriff answered, close behind him. Conscious how they had switched roles he added, "Too much, I'm afraid. Unless they're fools."

"Aw, they gets careless sometimes"

"I never saw any this careless."

But Hunnicutt led doggedly on, descending now, and soon they were in the hollow walking beside the branch. After a few moments they could see the lake down ahead. "There you are," the sheriff said.

They stood gazing at the boat drawn up at the water's edge. It was not even the same boat; it was much smaller, homemade, a flat-bottom skiff large enough only for fishing. And there inside were a cane pole and a rusty bait can. Smart, the sheriff thought; and he felt mingled with his relief a dim glow of admiration. For Flint? The thought gave a little jolt to his perspective, a shift that clearly brought to mind the image of himself standing here with the Honest Sheriff's face beside his deputy, his enemy, saying, "I told you they couldn't be that big a fools."

The sound of his own voice righted him. He knew he had made another slip, knew it even before he heard the obstinate voice of Hunnicutt reply, "Yeah. Well, you can't never be too sure." The sheriff did not answer. He pretended to search the bank with his eyes but really it was Hunnicutt whom he watched—Hunnicutt standing still in his tracks, gazing up and down the misty cove.

"Come on. It's sure not out there in the water," the sheriff said brusquely, and turned and started back up the hollow. But after a little he paused, for he did not hear any footsteps behind him. A glance showed him that Hunnicutt had turned, was following now; but he seemed in no hurry and his face was half screened under the wide brim of his hat. Moving on, the sheriff said in a tone he had to force, "We better hustle. I want to get done out here before night."

He had calculated his time almost exactly. In the faint gray of daylight they came down into the hollow at a safe distance above the mill. The sheriff, with pretense of divining his direction, led them south up the hollow and up the slope to the highway in the dark. This was just as he had planned it. In fact, except for those moments near the house and this other down beside the lake, the thing had gone off exactly as intended. But these, and mainly the last one, continued to disturb him. Driving back to town he said, "Well, looks like you were right this time. It seemed like as good a bet as any, though."

"Yep," Hunnicutt said, and that was all.

Given his natural sulkiness, this brevity need have meant nothing whatever. But the sheriff had expected to hear him gloat. There was no way to pursue it further, however, and he drove on back to town in troubled silence, in the rainy night.

That night was a bad one for the sheriff. Without his family there, the house had all the dank and hollow stillness of one vacant for a long time. It faintly echoed his footsteps, drowned his silences. He even fancied that he saw on the mute tops of tables and arms of chairs ghostly dust palls already forming. All because, he told himself, for once he felt tired to exhaustion. But he was glad of this: he would bury himself in sleep. He left the house unheated and trudged up the steps to his bedroom. There was sound here, the gentle, thought-diminishing sound of rain on the roof. Huddling under his covers he waited for the stroke of sleep.

What came upon him instead was like a daze, in which the rain continued to sound and his thoughts ran as free as dreams. Images came in confusion: Sibyl rocking in the chair, Hazel with her cheek that brushed like snow across his lips. Hazel again, but cheeks bright now with a flush that made his lips tingle. His tingling body, wrapped and fused with hers. In tinted light, as from the windows of a church. It was spring down the valley and the land a rich crimson with acres of blooming clover. An apple orchard in bloom. A cow with swollen udder, dripping milk; and earth flowing in a black stream across the bright plowsteel. Soft rain. It went on falling, without a break, and made the distance gray. He could see the flash of Alma's white arm working the pump. Hunnicutt with a smirk: "We might ought to just drop in some morning and make a little company for her."

It was just as if that voice had brought the sheriff suddenly wide awake. He found he was sweating under the heap of covers. Maybe a man could not sweat with hatred, but it seemed to the sheriff then that precisely his hatred was the cause of it. Lying in the darkness and the sound of steady rain he could not form in his mind any epithet vile enough for Hunnicutt. The countless acts of petty viciousness, the hateful gestures, the malice in his words and in his eyes: these came flocking into the sheriff's mind. And that smirk— how many times had he seen it appear in the obscene face suspended above a picture magazine? The sheriff's fingers tensed with the memories. And then he envisioned Hunnicutt standing on the lake bank with a certain astuteness of expression.

This last image caused the sheriff finally to rise up onto

his elbow and to remain for a long time propped this way with the air cold on his damp skin. He would have to go and warn them—now; he got half out of the bed. But his car was parked by the office door, and Pollard, on duty, would notice. Tomorrow, then, as early as he could—it would have to do. Most likely, anyhow, Hunnicutt had guessed nothing. Hunnicutt. He tried to shut his memory against that face. He managed it at last by fixing his mind on Alma.

VI

_____

THE SHERIFF FOUND a chance the next day at noon and made a hurried trip. She was in the muddy yard behind the house, hanging clothes on a wire in the bright intermittent sunshine.

"I'm not sure, of course," the sheriff said. "Probably it didn't mean anything. But it might. I can't control him."

From the way she looked off across the pasture while he spoke she might not have been listening. Then she said, "Don't he work for you?"

There was a coolness, or maybe something more, that distressed him. "Yes. But I told you about him. I can't keep him on a leash—you understand that. I told you he hates me." The sheriff heard, as he finished, the pleading tone in his voice.

"How come you don't fire him?"

"I'd have to have a good reason. You know I couldn't right now, anyway." The sheriff had made his voice more firm. Still she looked across the pasture; the sunshine came and went on her face and on her rich disordered hair. He made himself say, "They still haven't moved it out of there, have they?"

"Ain't you been to see?" she said indifferently.

"No. You know I haven't." He hesitated. "But they haven't

moved it, have they? Tell them they'll have to now, quick. It's just too big a risk. I'll try to keep him busy the next couple of days, but I can't forever."

"All right." She began again to hang up clothes on the wire.

After a moment: "Don't you see? They've *got* to."

"I said, all right."

The anger that started up in him gave way to a certain inchoate panicky feeling. He watched her go on hanging the clothes, moving farther away from him down the wire; watched how her up-reaching arms drew taut the shirt across the swell of her breasts. With effort he said, "Can I come tonight?"

"Better not tonight."

That feeling was gathered tight around his heart. He realized then—it was the first time he really had—how firmly, and consciously, she had him hooked. But he only closed his eyes again and said, "All right. When?"

"Oh I can't tell. In a few days, maybe."

And this was all he got. He tried for a minute more, and finally drove away with the same tightness around his heart. But even then he did not allow himself to dwell on it or to consider carefully whether he now could, if he wanted, unsnare himself. He deliberately fastened his gaze upon only what lay dead ahead. The thing now was to divert Hunnicutt: this was what she had clearly meant by her coldness. But if Hunnicutt was suspicious, then it could not be done for long. Surely she would see this; she must. Or Flint would if she did not, and get the still out quick.

Then, when it was done, what about Alma and himself?

He quickly put this out of mind and turned his attention to Hunnicutt. The rest of that day was no problem, for Hunnicutt was on duty until night. And so would he be the next day, until noon. That night, in his sleeplessness, the

sheriff thought of a way: he would send Hunnicutt down to
Finch on the Sutton case. And it did not displease him to
anticipate the sullen response, exactly the one he got from
Hunnicutt next morning.

"How come you or Pollard can't? I'm supposed to be off."

"I've got to see Judge Cate at three. And you know the
people. You can get off all day Saturday instead."

Glaring past him Hunnicutt said, "I got things to do
today."

The sheriff almost said, "What things?" and caught himself. He said, "You can do them Saturday." It was then that
he noticed, stretched suggestively out across both pages of
Hunnicutt's open magazine, the picture of a naked woman.
It faintly jolted him at first; then he was conscious of Hunnicutt's hard green gaze on him. To conceal his flush of
hatred the sheriff abruptly turned and walked away and
only afterward said, from across the office, "You can get back
by supper time."

It was another small failure of control on the sheriff's part.
In addition to a fear that Hunnicutt might have made some
vaguely meaningful surmise from it, he felt a sort of unrea-
soning jealousy: he had not forgotten Hunnicutt's smirk and
his words directed at Alma. At any rate, his emotion toward
Hunnicutt was such that he could not be sure of concealing
it. He left the office shortly and did not come back until past
noon, when he knew that Hunnicutt would be gone.

Later, especially after Bascomb stopped in, he was feeling
a great deal more at ease. Bascomb had unearthed nothing;
in fact he was ready to give up on Rhine County and move
on into Finch. This determined the sheriff to say nothing
about McCain. He thought it enough to say merely, while
Bascomb serenely sat twirling his key chain, "We've looked
everywhere we can think of. Not a thing. Not even a one-
potter."

He thought afterward, with just a fleeting moment of astonishment, that for the Honest Sheriff this had been a quite professional performance. But he felt greatly reassured; he even felt it most unlikely that Hunnicutt suspected anything. And now if Flint *was* doing as he had been told—if he did, as was probable, move it to some new and unknown location—then . . .? The sheriff's thinking ran out in a sudden desolate pause. From this came his vision of Alma, and then a flash of desire that was like pain in his bowels. Tonight he would go to the mill and see. And not *be* seen: somehow he felt better not throwing his own weight in the balance.

At seven o'clock he was in the office alone, pondering whether, when Pollard came back on duty, he would or would not go out to the mill. The telephone rang. It was Ethel Hunnicutt, a voice as colorless and dry and downcast as the small woman who in his mind's eye stood timidly gripping the receiver with both her hands. She didn't like to bother him but she wanted to know—she wondered if maybe he knowed—where Ralph was. For several seconds the sheriff did not reply; then he was distantly conscious of her voice patiently reproducing the whole rigmarole. He answered her this time, but even after the click and the steady humming sounded in his ear he did not put the receiver down. He never did: he called long-distance to Finch, to attorney Elmer Tate. No, Tate's voice boomed at him; no, he had not been there. And a second call, to Sutton, got the same reply. One thing was clear: Hunnicutt had not been to Finch that afternoon.

The sheriff sat gripping the arms of his chair, watching the sweep of the second-hand around and around the face of the wall clock. Beneath the clock were faces that did not tell anything, the empty staring ones of the "wanted" men. There were footsteps outside. The sheriff, seeing the figure of Pollard loom at the door, tried to compose himself. He started: in his ears was a squawking static from the radio on the counter.

Pollard stood behind him, listening with him, while from the speaker the patrolman's voice came wavering, as ragged as a snarl. Afterward there was silence. "What the heck?" Pollard said. The long narrow face, no less gloomy for the question in it, met the sheriff as he turned. Brushing past him the sheriff said, "I better get out there."

"What you reckon could have happened to him?"

But the sheriff went straight for the door and out and set the car in motion with a lurch. He ran the traffic lights; already speeding, he hit the Nashville highway. Not the Finch but the Nashville highway—an empty patrol car pulled off into a dirt side road. It took the sheriff, driving fast, maybe a long ten minutes. There were two patrol cars parked and a nervous beam of light that kept shifting up and down the side road. Patrolman Mullins came to meet him.

"Just happened to spot it in there. About forty-five minutes ago. No sign of anybody."

"You're sure he's not around someplace?" the sheriff said.

"Don't see how. We looked everywhere. And holloed. Blowed the horn. Ain't a house in a mile."

"Nothing about the car?"

"Not a thing. You say he was supposed to be gone to Finch?"

"Yes." The sheriff walked down the side road to the parked car, where three patrolmen stood in the dark conversing murmurously. He responded vaguely to them. With Mullins's light he leaned in through a window. The keys were in the switch. There was nothing, in the front, in the back, on the floor; in the dashboard pocket were a flashlight and the car documents in a leather wallet. "You didn't find a thing?"

"Sure didn't. We looked her over good, too," Mullins said.

Shining the light, bending to peer underneath as he went, the sheriff circled the car. There was nothing to see—no bits of vegetation clinging, no mud that looked fresh. He thought, in fact, that the wheels and undercarriage seemed cleaner than usual. He switched the light off and stood with his thoughts tumbling one over another. In the end they were all one thought, the same he had had before, and now it grew quite static in his head. Fireflies winked among the trees in the thicket; there were crickets and cicadas, and the air seemed oppressive with a musty scent of some blooming weed nearby.

"Way I figure it, Hunnicutt ain't been around here," Mullins said. "Somebody drove his car down here to hide their tracks. Plenty of people had it in for Hunnicutt."

There was a murmur from the darkness where the other patrolmen stood.

"Could be," the sheriff mumbled. He thought a moment. "I'll lock it up and leave it here till morning; we might have overlooked something. We'll go over it good then—if nothing's turned up." He had to say more. "Mullins, you drive on down toward Finch. Ask around. You all do the same on this road, Dale." He said these things in a flat automatic voice—and all for show.

But how could he be so certain? he thought, lunging against the mood of oppression that held him like a sickness as he drove back. Plenty of people, as Mullins had said, had it in for Hunnicutt. And the sheriff himself had warned him against those private searches: it might have happened at any of several places. If, indeed, this was not a freak and Hunnicutt did not turn up as always. Yes, he might be there in the morning, at his desk, leering down with his obscene face at a nude in his magazine.

But these reflections did not help much. He had to compose himself, his expression, before he dared get out of his car and walk to the office door where Pollard waited.

"No sign of him. Just the car."

"He couldn't be snooping around there someplace?"

"There's nothing to snoop around along there. Keys in the car."

Pollard watched him dismally. "What do you reckon?"

The sheriff walked to his desk and stood with his back to Pollard. "I don't know."

"Maybe some moonshiner. Or one of them people he's roughed up."

"Maybe." The sheriff slid the tips of his fingers back and forth on the polished surface of his desk. A noise made him look up sharply, a curious and eerie noise that left an echo in his head. "What was that?"

"Oh, just old Dobbs back there. Having him a dream."

The sheriff looked at the dark doorway into the cell block. A place for dreaming, he thought. "He's all right, isn't he?"

"Yeah, I reckon. Same as always. By the way, Hunnicutt's old lady wants you to call her."

"You call her for me," the sheriff said, and turned and walked straight to the door.

"Hey, where you going to be?"

"Out looking," the sheriff answered and let the screen door clap shut behind him.

Lightning flickered among clouds to the southwest. Drops of rain had begun to pelt his windshield before he pulled to a stop near the mouth of the log road. There were faint wheel tracks, all right—he could trace them in his flashlight beam through the weeds and brush—but he could not be sure they were newly made. He was out again with his light where the muddy road turned off to Alma's. And again there were tracks. Whose tracks? He remembered how the under-carriage of Hunnicutt's car had looked nearly clean, as if it had passed recently through water; and he thought again of the ford on Bracken Pike which connected this highway and that to Nashville. By now the rain was falling fast. In the darkness of his car he sat and gazed in front of him at the dim rain-blinded windshield. Decision took him all at once.

He drove straight up to the house and stopped beside the battered car that was parked almost at the foot of the steps. There was light in the house, but no sound. He did not try to soften his footfalls as he climbed the steps, nor did he restrain the force of his knuckles against the heavy door panel. Too loud, he thought, hearing his knock resound inside the house. He had not even glanced in through the window light; now he did. Through the dusty pane he saw them all, seated, their faces like so many masks of wood or stone chiseled in one common rigid stare. The next instant Flint was getting to his feet, and the sheriff stepped back.

The door opened, but only wide enough to frame exactly the two shadowy deep-set eyes. For a moment it appeared that Flint could not even see through the crack the figure squarely facing him. The door opened wider, exposing the whole width of the massive face and body, releasing the voice: "Well. Sheriff Tawes." The faint unpleasant lisp at the end was like the escape of pressure from his lips. "Come on in, Sheriff . . . away from all that rain."

Their common stare fastened upon him. "Reptilian" now, instead of wooden, was the word that flitted through his mind. He had already noticed that Alma, in this brief interval, had vanished from the room. What he noticed with greater impact was a fourth man seated on the floor with his back to the door jamb. Perhaps it was this position, the darkness of that particular room in back of him over his shoulder, that struck the sheriff so: he imagined the same face staring hard out of that darkness at him.

"Well, set down, Sheriff. There's a chair right there," Flint was saying, lisping, at his side. Then, "That there's Leo Carp. He's a friend of our'n. You know my boys a'ready."

The boys, at angular sprawling postures on the ruined sofa, acknowledged nothing at all. Neither did Leo Carp, seated behind, his knees against the door jamb. It was hard to see him plainly in the lamplight; it was clear only that he had pale ankles, sparse backswept hair, and a blunt hard-featured face. And one thing more: despite his easy posture, a look of strain, like a man pretending not to be cornered.

"I reckon you come to see Alma, though, didn't you?"

The words, as if they had been shouted, released the sheriff from his trance. "No, I didn't." He found himself now cool enough to wait for the effect. But there was no effect.

"All right, then. You want to set—"

"I want to know where Hunnicutt is. My deputy."

They all—all but Flint—had been so still before that he could not observe any difference in them. The only difference was in Flint, who now had joined them in their stillness; there was a moment in which that clock began unmistakably to tick. But Flint swept this away as if it had not been. "I don't reckon we know him, Sheriff." With a glance at the others: "You know him, boys?" Snake shook his head; the other two did not. "I'm afraid we can't help you none there, Sheriff. He ain't been out around here, has he?"

"He came out here this afternoon," the sheriff said with all the assurance he could manage.

Flint shook his big head sagely. "Well, if he did, and he never went back, he's still poking around out there in the rain someplace."

The sheriff regarded the placid expression; then a small light came on in his mind. "Doesn't that make you uneasy?"

"Sure it does. But you're the onliest one can do anything. I was just thinking oughtn't you be out seeing about him."

The sheriff looked away, to where the boys on the sofa

and Carp propped against the jamb watched him like gazing dummies. "We found his car down on the Nashville highway tonight. Somebody besides him drove it down there."

"Did they, now?" Flint said. There was no ring of irony, there was every show of real wonderment in his voice. "But what I can't figure, Sheriff, is how come you're looking for him out here."

It was much too thick, as always. Flint's hand, expressing bewilderment in just the fitting degree, came up and stroked the stubble on his bulging cheekbone. " 'Cause we surely ain't seen him. We ain't seen nobody. We never even got home from work till late."

The sheriff's gaze had picked up something—mud on Ed's shoes. There was even mud on his trouser leg. The sheriff's eyes made a quick circuit of all their shoes. All were muddy, including Flint's. But Flint had noticed too. "Aw, we got home in time to go down to the mill for a little spell." Then he added, "We're getting it all cleared out down there now, Sheriff. Like you said to. We'll be through pretty quick now. Won't none of us have no worry then."

The sheriff only looked at him. Flint could not think that he believed this. Did he also know that the sheriff believed nothing of what he had said? Once again the sheriff had that sense of being read more deeply than he could read himself. Those mute stares were growing intolerable. What had he intended by bursting in this way? What did he now intend to do, for wouldn't any bluffing declaration be merely ludicrous?

Flint's voice, his unctuous lisping voice, was there like a sudden balm on the sheriff's desperation. "You're just upset, Sheriff. Blaming yourself for something. And don't even know for sure yet it's nothing wrong. You go in there and talk to Alma. It ain't nothing like having a woman by when you're all upset."

In that moment this seemed an escape for the sheriff; he felt toward Flint a sudden irrational gratitude—exactly as though the sympathy were real, as though a father's voice had shown his way out. Then, in the stare of all their eyes, he felt an uprush of shame. He gathered himself to speak, but Flint interrupted: "You boys clear out of here."

"I didn't come to see Alma," the sheriff burst out.

"I said 'get.'"

They were already on their feet, in the same wooden silence turning away like puppets driven by the old man's voice.

"I didn't come to see Alma," the sheriff repeated with the same force.

But the boys passed on, up the stairs, disappearing into the gloom that thickened around them as they climbed. The sheriff had a feeling of helplessness, like protesting in a dream. He heard a door upstairs fall shut. He heard the clock, and then the rain.

"Alma," Flint called out.

She was already standing in the kitchen doorway, looking at them. Then Flint was gone. It was nearly as if he had vanished; only in the last moment did the sheriff glimpse him in the darkness of the next room with his hand already swinging the door across his silhouette. Then this door too was closed, and there was rain. There was a strange feeling in the way Alma looked at him.

"You want a cup of coffee?"

Her voice brought a certain firmness back to things. He crossed the room and entered the kitchen door near the stairs. Already she was standing, with her back to him, before the wood stove at the other end of the low dim kitchen.

"You better set down," she said, as if she could see that he had not and, in fact, did not mean to. But he did sit down.

A low-burning lamp stood on the table, on a stained once-yellow oilcloth. It was so close to where he had sat down that he could feel the heat, and he pushed it away. The flame reeled and this made shadows in far-off corners and overhead in the rafters quake. There was a beard of peppers hanging. Then it seemed to him that this beard of peppers was familiar. And so were other things around the room: wood-box, wash-tub by the door, the big black stove where a woman stood with her back to him. Named Alma, he thought, half in surprise, for it came to mind with the air of a name he had conjured up himself.

At this moment she came toward him with two steaming china mugs in her hands. He found himself staring hard at her face, searching it. Searching for what? It took him a moment to realize that he was looking there for signs of agitation, for a slight pallor, maybe, or an evasiveness in her eyes. But he could see nothing, not even when she sat down in the lamplight directly across from him. A surliness, perhaps? Or was it only the unaccustomed angle from which he saw her face, which made her jaw and even her mouth look rude and harsh? He did not like the look; he lowered his gaze to the steaming cup of coffee as black as ink. Except for the rain there was no sound anywhere.

"I never told you to come tonight," she said sullenly.

He did not look up. "Don't you know why I did?"

"I heard you talking."

"Then you know why."

She was silent for a moment. "I'd of thought you'd be glad to get rid of him."

Now he looked at her, stared at her, seeing the same hardness of mouth and jaw, seeing her lift the cup and sip gingerly at the hot coffee. Just above a whisper he said, "Am I rid of him?"

She set the cup down attentively. "I don't know about

that. We ain't seen him. We ain't seen anybody. You're the one said it first."

He supposed he had said it first—or implied it. But there was a vaguely sick feeling deep down in his belly, and the coffee before him now appeared like so much smoking tar in the cup. At length: "Why did you think I'd be glad?"

"'Cause of what you told me about him. How you hated him. And couldn't get rid of him."

"When did I ever tell you that?"

"Yesterday. When you come out here. And before that, too."

"No I didn't; I didn't say that. I said he hated *me*. And that I couldn't fire him now." This was all he had said—nothing else. He added, "That's all I told you. You know that."

Now she looked at him, shifted only her eyes to do it. He was struck first of all with how hard they looked, with little diamond points of lamplight in the gray. Then he saw the scorn, the contempt in all her face. For a moment he willed himself to meet it squarely. But the sickness growing in his belly seemed to undermine his force, and the anger he tried to summon would not come. He looked down, like a child. All he could think to say, weakly, was, "You know that."

"I know what you told me," her cold voice replied.

He did not try to answer and he did not look up again until he heard her move to lift her cup. She was sipping coffee with her hard mouth, a mouth he did not know. She was someone else, he vaguely thought; and this place, this obscurely familiar kitchen, was the very womb of desolation. He listened to steady rain on the roof, to water sluicing down from the eaves. He fancied it gathering into a flood, rising up the walls and over the eaves until all was submerged at last, intact, with lamp burning and silence complete and no longer any way out. He would get up and leave now.

He did take his arm off the table. What arrested him was the thought of her room upstairs, with tinted light from the turret door falling into the darkness around her bed. Then, curiously, he thought of Flint, thought of calling him to come and set things right, to change her back into the warm and passionate body which he now knew his sickness was only the yearning for. But he took another look at her. He stirred and then got numbly to his feet.

"You needn't to go," she suddenly said.

He did not answer.

"You ain't even drunk your coffee."

"I don't want it." But he had paused. Outside the rain kept falling.

"I ain't mad at you. You're just all upset; that's all."

With confusion of desire and shame, he knew that it was her altered tone which had stopped him. He looked at her with an overwhelming sense of his helplessness. Then, faintly, she smiled. At once the softness was there on her mouth again.

"I wish you'd stay a while with me," she murmured.

He instantly knew how meaningless was his puny attempt to say no. His sense of deep humiliation was quite smothered in the surge of his desire when he saw her rise and come toward him around the table.

VII

―――――

"**N**OTHING," POLLARD SAID gloomily when the sheriff got back to the office that night. And later on, the same report came in from patrolmen Mullins and Dale. When morning still had brought nothing new the sheriff no longer nursed any hope that Hunnicutt would appear. Hunnicutt was dead. Then another thing also was clear. Someone had killed him. The sheriff leaned far back in his swivel chair and shut his lids against the early sunshine that streamed from a window into the throbbing sockets of his eyes. He sat this way for a long time, in a state of mental suspension nearly like sleep. When at last a clear thought did take shape in his mind, it concerned the enemies that Hunnicutt had made. Deliberately he fixed his attention on this and tried to remember who they were and which of these had boldness enough for the act. Getting up from his chair, he stepped quickly to the file cabinet. For some time he was turning through ledgers, marking, considering cases with an intentness that shut out other thoughts. He contemplated even the most doubtful cases, and when he was done he had nearly a score of names.

So, forcing all his energies into play, he launched the investigation. He minutely examined Hunnicutt's car, and found nothing; whoever had driven it there had not been a careless person. The sheriff's next move was to deputize a number of men and send them, in pairs, to search about the premises of all the people he had marked. For it might have been any one of these. In fact the sheriff personally went searching once, in the company of a boy named Rawson. And not without a good deal of hope, he told himself; for the run-down backwoods farm just off the Finch highway belonged to an inveterate and vicious moonshiner, Caleb Stock, whom Hunnicutt not only had twice arrested but one of these times had wounded for resisting. It came to nothing. Stock sneered at them: he had been at Finch yesterday and far into the night and he could prove it. This was the only time the sheriff went out in person; for the face-to-face destruction of this particular hope seemed momentarily to bring down the whole enterprise like so much rubble falling around him.

Other things, however, also shook him. One of these was a report that Hunnicutt, on the afternoon in question, had been seen driving out the Gatesboro highway, the road to Alma's. But other reports followed: Hunnicutt had been seen on other highways too, going in different directions at once. Besides, the car he had been driving was in no way distinguishable from the other patrol cars. So this, at least, passed over. Ethel Hunnicutt, her gray, subdued, apologetic voice coming to him every few hours over the telephone, could not be so dismissed. Always her calls rattled him. His answer quickly settled down to a ritual: "No ma'am. I'm sorry. Nothing yet. We'll let you know right away when we do." Lest he stumble he made himself run fast across that "when." But what disturbed him most was to be reminded each time of a perfectly uncomplicated fact: Hunnicutt had had a wife, and one who cared about him.

But nothing really stuck with the sheriff for long. Through

the busy days that followed he managed to keep almost intact the illusion of a good conscience in this matter. As for the eyes of his colleagues, he believed that nothing in his manner or his actions pointed to a troubled spirit; the air of authority natural to him went virtually undiminished. What happened finally, and did change all this overnight, was something that did not have to do with Hunnicutt.

It had now been four days since Hunnicutt's disappearance, and since that night—that hour whose remembrance inflamed him still—the sheriff had not seen Alma. This was not because circumstances had made it impossible. And certainly it was not because there was any waning of his desire for her. It fact, now, she was almost constantly somewhere in his thoughts, haunting chambers where he would not have expected to find her. "Obsession," he supposed, was the proper word. But whatever it ought to be called, he knew that the image of her was the one thing he could no longer afford to be without. For it seemed to him the source not only of his passion but even of those puny energies that daily life required of him. Thoughts of her there in the tinted light of her room came like a tide in which he could immerse and refresh himself. The sheriff's reason, then, for having stayed away these last four days was quite another kind of thing. He knew dimly that it was fear—a fear he did not allow himself to scrutinize at all. Or had not until now, when this happened.

It was in the afternoon as he stood at the head of the steps that mounted onto the courthouse walk. Bascomb was beside him. At the foot of the steps was Pitt, the district attorney, who kept punctuating his remarks with quick impatient shakes of his head. Right now he was saying, looking up at Bascomb, "There's nothing to follow up. If he just hadn't been so damned secretive."

For at least the third time Bascomb said, "I just *keep* knowing it was that bunch I'm after. He had got onto them some way."

"Maybe," the sheriff said. "It could have been a lot of people, though, the way things were." He was not especially conscious just then of defending anything, either within or outside of himself. After some twenty minutes of talking with them like this he had reached one of those peaks of confidence when it seemed to him that he really was all that he pretended to be. Otherwise, perhaps, he might have noticed sooner.

He was standing at some two feet of elevation above the wide street in front of him, directly facing the polished tile and glass front of Digby's hardware store. There was movement everywhere: traffic surged and halted, and over on the sidewalk people in an intermittent stream passed across the bright store front. But there was one man who did not move. The sheriff now realized that the man had been standing over there, his back to the wall, for at least as long as the sheriff had been here. And, seemingly without the least break, he had been all this time watching the threesome across the street. It then occurred to the sheriff that only he was being watched, and in that moment a cloud came over the sun. This sudden shrouding of the light seemed to be the reason that his nerves went instantly taut. He was now staring directly back, but without causing the man over there to falter. Still it was no summons, the sheriff concluded; the man had not tried to draw his attention. Then there was something familiar to the sheriff, like the nearly forgotten feel of an old embrace. Somewhere, he vaguely felt, he and that man had locked eyes this way before. He did not know exactly when or how the recognition came that the man was Leo Carp.

"Do you know anything else to try?"

The sheriff realized that this was the second time the question had been asked and he had to force his attention back to the conversation. When again he found space for a glance across the street, he saw that Carp was gone.

When the others had left, the sheriff stayed where he was and searched the square with his eyes. At length he crossed the street and stood where Carp had and—while the people and traffic passed by and the warm spring sunlight came and went—gazed back over at the spot where he himself had been standing. Maybe from here, in Carp's tracks, he could better understand what had been in Carp's mind. Certainly it had not been a summons, for Carp had left. Some sort of a challenge, maybe: there had seemed to be a suggestion of that. But a challenge to what? Or maybe there was no meaning at all except that Carp's involvement gave him an interest in the sheriff. This was the view that the sheriff favored and tried to settle for. In fact, with this in his head, he turned away and went about his business again.

But not for very long. Though he kept thrusting it away the question came back each time with an intensity that at last set his mind smoldering. Who *was* Leo Carp? He could connect the name with nothing; certainly it was not one that belonged to this part of the country. Dredging among his memories he could bring up, kept bringing up, only this single fact: Alma used to have a husband.

Alone in his office the sheriff paced from wall to wall, pausing only now and then by windows to stare with empty eyes out into the street. At length he stopped at the file cabinet. The minutes he spent turning through old records produced, as he had expected, no such name. But they did produce something, and for another minute or two he stood pointlessly observing how the soiled folder beneath his fingertips seemed to quiver with a life of its own. He did not think until afterward, after he had thrust the drawer shut and picked up his hat and stepped out onto the sidewalk, that he was leaving the office unattended. It did not stop him. More hurriedly than he should have done he turned his car around and drove away up the block.

Later, as he turned off the highway, it occurred to him that he had even neglected to glance behind for any car that might have been in sight. Still he did not look back. He would confront her with it, squarely. His car went jogging down the rutted dirt road and soon there was the turret, the house.

The house was deserted. In the cool stillness of the big living room he stood and called out, with echoes dying up above. He even climbed the steps to her empty room. The woods, the mill—where else could she be? He left the house walking fast, crossed the pasture, and followed the path that led down through the beech woods. Two or three times he paused and called out among the trees, and got no answer. There was no one at the mill either. He peered down through the trap door, noticing that there was not any change in the still, nothing moved from its place.

Back at the house again, sweating, he stood inside the door and listened while the stillness wrapped him deeper and deeper until it seemed to smother the sound of his breath. One more time, pointlessly, he called out, "Alma." In the soundless aftermath of his voice came a feeling of desperation like a spur. He moved out of his tracks, and only then realized that he did have an intention. He wrote a note. On the rough table top where the lamp stood, on a sheet of paper he had to smooth out with his hand, he watched himself write:

I want you to marry me. We can keep it secret for a while, then go away. If the things you told me are really true. Are they true?

He stopped. He thought for a brief moment of scratching out this last . . . or all of it. Throw it away, for none of it made sense. Instead he added:

I will get a divorce from my wife right away. I want your promise. I'll come back tonight.

It made no sense. He took the paper and crumpled it in his hand. But after some moments of standing there staring at his knotted fist, his white knuckles, he opened his hand and once more straightened the paper out. With impulsive haste he started walking, climbed the stairs, and placed the note on the pillow of her bed.

He drove swiftly toward Gatesboro, in a state of mind that kept evading every substantial thought. Even when, at dusk, he turned the last corner he had not yet come to grips with his intention. Then it was too late, for there, crowded in among billowing shrubs, was the house. He saw Hazel. She was standing with a look of repose, sprinkling a border of flower beds, spray from the nozzle in her hand catching silver in the last daylight. The vision made something abrupt happen in the sheriff's mind. At a stop now, he sat watching her from the car window, hearing the hush of the silver spray and last birds settling down in a tree somewhere. It was as if a door just behind him had fallen shut on some nightmare interior that had enclosed him until now, and he was restored to a world of spray and twittering birds at dusk.

But his wife was looking at him, he saw. Slowly he got out of the car and then he saw her drop the hose and step across the yard to where the spigot was. She straightened up as he came in at the gate; her wan face gazed through the twilight at him. With still a little distance between them, he stopped. He wanted this to last; he listened to the birds. But soon, unsettled by her stillness, he had to speak.

"I wanted to talk to you." About what? he thought, a thought that vaguely suggested a distant shrill alarm.

"All right." She walked to where three yard chairs were set under a small maple tree, and he noted how the dusky light softened the angles of her body. They sat; they watched a car pass by on the street. Since all words kept eluding him anyway and he felt tired and curiously at rest, he was wishing that this silence might last on and on.

She said, "I heard about Mr. Hunnicutt. Not from you."

He breathed deep. His languor was gone like a dream.

"You still haven't found him?"

"No," he mumbled, glad for the darkness under the tree. "Nothing at all. Yet," he added faintly.

A pause. "What could have happened?" It was a flat tone, not the tone of inquiry.

"We don't know." Maybe a minute went by this way.

"What did you come for?"

All he could manage was, "I wanted to talk to you."

She waited, very still, blurring out in the gathering dark. Evidently she intended, no matter how long it took, to wait him out. Still he did not speak. How could he, when he never had given the matter even a minute's rational thought?

She surprised him:

"I think I can guess what."

He hung in her pause.

"You want a divorce. Is that right?"

He tried to swallow back the constriction in his throat. Was this really what he wanted?

"Is that right?" she repeated.

He murmured, "Yes."

"Because you've got another woman."

For a long time he could think of no reply. Indeed, because of the tightness in his throat, he could not have given any. But he knew now that at least a part of this emotion that bound him so was shame. "Why do you think that?"

"I'm not a fool."

"Did somebody tell you that?"

"No. It's true, isn't it?"

When finally it came, not even he could hear his whispered "Yes." Nevertheless it was as if she had heard, for she said:

"I knew it was. I don't suppose you want to tell me . . . who it is."

"It's . . . not anybody you know."

She was silent, holding her dim hands one upon the other on her lap. It must have been a long time ago the last birds had hushed.

"I suppose the sooner the better," she said. "I'll see Fred Herron tomorrow."

But what would this lead to? He had a sudden benumbing consciousness of his folly; he started to say something, he did not know what. Later he tried to say, "I'm sorry," but this would not come out either. It was she who released him finally, by standing up.

After that it was over quickly. One broken utterance of regret from him, her silence, an inquiry or two, and he was left standing in the yard alone. Even then no light came on in the house. He lingered at the gate, thinking of his daughter. Suddenly, lest she appear, he got into his car and drove away down the street.

And the thing was done; without his even planning it, even thinking it through, it was done. He considered this fact with some confusion, almost as though it were not his own doing. He felt very strange to himself, and this unfamiliar street he followed, taking him he did not know where, seemed only to support his feeling of disorientation. Once he said out loud, "Hank Tawes," but the sound of his own name made no difference. Then the street dead-ended.

To avoid driving back by the house he took the first turn left, and two blocks on, another turn. There were neon lights, cars crossing an intersection. It was exactly as if his mind had suddenly untilted; things in all their urgency snapped back into a pattern. He was on the highway again, driving fast, then too fast, so that he forced himself to lighten the weight of his foot on the pedal. Behind him something final had been done. Was that what he had really wanted? It seemed to be so—at some depth of himself that he was no longer even curious about. Already there was no room left in his mind for any other matter than the one ahead of him.

He was driving so fast, with such impatience, that he had to brake the car hard in order to make the turn onto the dirt road. As soon as he came into the open he saw that there was no light in any window of the house, and then, in the beams of his headlights, that the battered automobile still was not there. All his violence failed him suddenly. Nevertheless he pulled up in front of the steps and got out. The full moon was shining, and in its pale refulgence everything —turreted house, meadow stretching away to black horizons of timber, cheeping of invisible killdees—had somehow the quality of a static and empty dream. He felt as if he could not summon blood enough to keep his heart in motion. Until he saw something stir.

A figure was moving out of the shadows on the porch. The next moment the sheriff saw that it was the slight sinuous body of Snake, descending the steps, approaching him. And then the voice, husky, "Alma left you this here," and his hand held out a folded sheet of paper.

"Where is she?" the sheriff said tensely, seizing the paper.

"Went down to Sorrel County. Said she couldn't wait no

longer for you." For one instant a glaze of moonlight rested on the dark surfaces of his eyes.

"When will she be back?"

"She never said."

With clumsy fingers the sheriff unfolded the sheet of paper. Though he turned to get the moon behind him the paper remained all one grayish blur. "Why did—" But when he looked up, Snake was gone. He hurriedly got into the car and switched on the light.

Sorry I can not wate for you, I got kin bad sick to go help out. You need not to worry all the things I said are true. I dont see why you dont think they are true. I want to marry you to. I promise because I love you. But we better be careful rite now because you getting a divorce from your wife on count of me is liable to give everything away. So jest wate a little while longer till things gets settled. It wont be long. I promise to marry you. Come back tomorrow nite and I will show you how much I love you.

Your sweethart Alma

He read it over three or four times, but it was only her last sentence that really fastened itself in his mind. In his body too, melting like something hot and sweet into his bloodstream. Nursing this, only this, he drove slowly back toward town, breathing through the open window cool odors from the woods, mingled scents of honeysuckle and wild violet and blooming locust. In town he drove past his office, saw Pollard seated inside under the light, and knew that he ought to stop in. Instead he kept on driving, slowly, through town and beyond and onto the winding road that followed the moonlit shore of the lake. Only after a long while, when he began to grow sleepy in the warmth of his own blood, did he turn his car toward home.

VIII

THE SHERIFF SLEPT heavily that night, and this time the dream he had did not end in panic, with straining lungs. Either he could breathe beneath the water or else he did not need to any longer. The filtered crystal light did not seem strange. There was even scent of apple blossoms in the orchard where he knelt, with his sisters, with knees rooted in the earth, with pale fingers weaving chains of daisies and crimson clover. The house was behind him; and so was the vague man's-figure whose presence kept everything intact. And this time his dream was merely dissolved in the rays of morning sunshine through his window.

He stretched himself in the bed. He knew the fragrant scent to mean that the locust trees in his back yard had bloomed overnight. Getting up, he stepped to the window for a look at them, at the tender foliage everywhere sprinkled with radiant flakes of white. Memories of a hundred spring mornings came rushing back, and he was gazing through trees up a valley washed emerald green and gold in the early sun. This day, in his haste to be dressed and outside, he scarcely noticed the stillness in his house.

Finches, darting from the bushes when he came out, made golden streaks on the air; and another bird, a thrush, sang from within the luminous green of the mimosa tree. He paused, with morning gladness in him, to look for the bird hidden, singing among the foliage. How very long since he had listened to a bird sing.

The day's business scarcely dimmed his glow of serenity; he even had intervals of near-conviction that nothing could touch him now. He was blameless, free. His thoughts kept running ahead, at a great distance from all this, drawn on by a hope that still remained as shapeless as a cloud. More than once he did not notice when Pollard first spoke to him, and at last he saw on Pollard's face a grin that must have meant something. He thought then that maybe, from Hunnicutt, Pollard had learned that he had a girl. But the thought gave him barely a twinge of anxiety. Neither did other things in this vein, things that only yesterday would have shaken him. There was the call from Ethel Hunnicutt, who wanted to see him, wanted to talk with him face to face. He put her off with forced gentleness. And another call, from Bascomb. It came while he was briefly out of the office, late in the afternoon, and these facts seemed excuse enough simply to forget until next morning.

He did forget it, too, entirely. In his mounting anticipation as night came on he a little resembled a mooning boy, absently drumming on his desk, pacing about the office. Pollard noticed and smirked again. The sheriff, to cover himself, uttered the first thing in his head: that he was going to Gatesboro to spend the night with his wife. He did not even pause to consider how this might sound to Pollard, for later he said it again. And it was the last, the only thing he said when Shanks, his new deputy, came on to relieve him that night at eight.

Tonight the battered car was there by the steps again. But even with this for assurance, as he stepped out into the moonlight something gave him pause. Some quality of the scene, perhaps the faint cries of the killdees, hovered sadly over his spirit in a moment of desolation. This lasted only a moment, however, in spite of the ghostly bird songs that followed him to the steps. These faded too as he mounted, lightly now, and approached the familiar door with hand already outstretched. No, he would not even knock. He simply opened the door himself and stepped into the lighted room.

He stopped. There were two people in the room, Flint and Leo Carp, and both had turned their heads to look at him. Only their heads: they had been facing each other and their bodies kept all the rigidity of duelists for a single moment diverted from their purpose. This was a first impression. Then he saw that Carp's back was to the wall, that for all his look of fierce malevolence his posture was vaguely defensive. At any rate Flint had no fear of him, for now he turned, turned his back on Carp to say, "Come on in, Sheriff. Been looking out for you. Alma's back there in the kitchen."

But his voice reflected strain. He must have been conscious of this, for he added, "Me and Leo here, we been having a little disagreement. Just 'tween friends. All over with, now." He looked back over his shoulder, waiting a moment for concurrence. It did not come. Instead Carp's gaze, a hot glare fastened until now on the sheriff, darted back to Flint and wavered and again returned to the sheriff. Flint also looked back at the sheriff, with something dying out of his face. "Leo, he's one of these hot-tempered kind."

The sheriff stood in his tracks, letting his eyes uncertainly shift from Flint to Carp again. A dryness had come like dust on his tongue. Flint moved, a turn toward the kitchen door. "Hey, Alma. Sheriff's here to see you."

No answer came. There was low lamplight through the door; and also, as he now saw, a shadow that stirred and then withdrew from sight.

"You go on back, Sheriff. She's busy back there."

Irrelevantly he thought of the open door behind him, and turning to shut it gave him a moment's release. This did not help; there were the eyes when he turned back, the tense waiting postures. There was something at which his mind balked. He felt unable to think what he should do and he simply went on standing there. Until Flint's voice, kindly, once more said, "You go on back. She's back there waiting for you."

He walked almost swiftly, feeling their eyes, around the table and straight to the kitchen door. Across the threshold he stopped. His gaze swept an empty room, darted from stove to looming cupboard, and settled at last on the door in the opposite wall. He knew, by the vertical hair of moon-light at its edge, that it stood faintly ajar. She had left it that way—fleeing him? He stood in the pale lamplight, under the low rafters, gazing at it. From the room behind him he barely heard the murmurous half-whispers of a voice. But there was passion in it. There were footfalls, next, and the sound of the front door opening. Then silence. And later, though the silence had drawn out like the fine humming of a wire inside his skull, he still had not moved from his tracks. His gaze now rested upon the familar beard of pep-pers hanging from the rafters. And now, too, other things seemed familiar—sounds like phantom footsteps around him in the house, and voices whose resonance was a tingling deep in the channels of his ears.

With sudden force he stalked across the kitchen, pulled the door open, and looked out into the moonlit yard. There was no one in sight. Only the sagging outbuildings with their shadows could have concealed a figure anywhere close by. Boards creaked when he stepped out onto the porch; he stopped in the bare back yard and called, "Alma," softly. There was no response, there were the faint shrill cries of the killdees, and he called again. If she was near she

heard him; he knew that. But there was no answer or movement anywhere.

There was movement out in the pasture. Some one was
walking out there, slowly, heading away from the house
toward the woods on the east side. He made out that it was
a man. Too slight for Flint. Then it was Carp. After a
moment the sheriff saw him pause, then wheel around as if
he intended violently to retrace his steps. He did not; he
continued the way he had started, quickly melting into the
wan distance.

What did it all mean? Almost unconsciously, as if to
escape an answer, he walked across the bare yard to the
shed. Peering into the shadows he called her name again—
only once, faintly. For it was no use; clearly she did not
mean for him to find her. Was this the end of it, then? The
thought of their last meeting in the kitchen, before her
abrupt change of mood, brought clearly to his mind's eye
that look of contempt in her face. And now, this.

He stood gazing across the field in the direction Carp had
gone—toward the mill. All at once he started walking, had
taken half a dozen steps in that direction before another
figure caught his eye. It was Flint—the sheriff could tell from
his bulk—leaning upon a post at a little distance from the
house. The sheriff hesitated; then, with decision, he walked
straight toward him.

Flint, looking out across the field, did not see him at first.
When he did, he wheeled, his eyes caught the moon, and a
curious rumbling noise issued from his chest. The sheriff
heard him draw breath, a breath that appeared to inflate
and straighten his body up again.

"Sheriff?" Flint said. Without waiting for an answer: "I
thought you was inside with Alma."

"No."

Flint was looking steadily at him. "How come you ain't?"

"Because she wasn't in there."

Flint paused again. "Wasn't, huh . . . Where's she at now?"

"I don't know. She went out when I came in the kitchen."

"Did, huh," Flint mumbled. He gazed toward the outbuildings. "Well, that ain't nothing. She'll be back in a minute."

"I don't think so," the sheriff said. "I think it's something to do with Carp. What about him?"

"Leo?" The way Flint turned his head then caused the moonlight to define all the bony protuberances of his face. "Nothing about him. Why?"

"Who is he?"

"Why, he's just Leo," Flint said, as if naming some common household item. "He helps us out some. He's a friend of my boys."

"He lives with you, doesn't he?"

"Yeah." Flint nodded weightily. "Yeah, part of the time he does. Ain't no harm in that, is they? We've all knowed Leo since he was a boy. What you worrying about him for?"

"What were you fighting with him about?"

"Aw, that. Wasn't nothing. Just a little argument."

"It was something about her."

Flint paused, raised a hand to scratch his cheek. There were faint cries of the killdees. "Alma? . . . Well, you're right," Flint said. "But it still ain't nothing. Leo, he's sweet on her. Mad at you 'cause he can't make no time with her. He got a little ugly this time."

The sheriff's first reaction was a feeling of deep relief. But almost instantly this passed. "Is that why she's treating me like this?"

Flint looked level at him. "You're all the time worrying, ain't you, Sheriff? And ain't got cause to. She's just upset about Leo cutting up. You know how gals is.... I'll tend to him."

In some uncertain way he was comforted by Flint's voice.
Just now he could scarcely remember what grounds he had
for doubt.

"You ain't got no worry, Sheriff," Flint said. "She's your
gal. Told me she aimed to marry you." And after a moment:
"You wait a minute. I'm going to go root her out for you."
Then he was walking away through the moonlight, moving
with deliberate strides and body stooped a little, toward the
nearest of the outbuildings. The sheriff saw him vanish in
the darkness under the shed. He heard his voice, easy and
slow, "Hey, Alma. Where you at, gal?" and saw him emerge
and then vanish again beyond the smokehouse.

The voice kept calling; and somehow, even at this distance, it was reassuring to the sheriff. Or was for a time.
Then—he was not at first sure why—his complacency started
to crumble. It was because of the voice, sounding with a
note of impatience now, hinting at something meaningful
and harsh beneath its restraint. He began only then to feel
a sense of humiliation, and also, with increasing distress, to
doubt what Flint had said. The sheriff stirred uneasily,
moved a step or two.

Flint was coming back in silence now, not toward him but
toward the back-porch steps. He was already climbing them
when he said, with a note that was still imperfectly sup-
pressed, "Must of gone back in. Take a look in her room,"
and then disappeared into the house. Of course she could
not be there. But even if she were, it would be no good this
way. How could he face her? Yet it was not this so much as
his other cause of distress that moved him, after an uncertain interval, abruptly to turn and hurry to his car.

He left his car in the log road off the highway and walked
swiftly down the hollow toward the mill. He still had no
plan, even when he had reached the place from where he

could see open sky and the dim palisade of grass ahead of him—or at least no plan except the hazy one of somehow confronting Carp and shaking the truth out of him. With his hands already spreading the tall grass before him he suddenly stopped. There was a voice. He sharply turned, but no one was behind him. From the millrace came the sound, louder than in the past, of rushing water. He heard the voice again—from behind the mill, it seemed, down on the water's edge. Cautiously he threaded his way through the grass to the foot of the wall and then down the incline to the rear corner.

At first, though he could more clearly hear voices, he saw nothing—only the moon's tattered reflection shimmering on the surface of the water below him. Then he did see something, on the water at the far corner of the mill. It was the stern of a large boat protruding out of the millrace there, shifting a little with the current. Below him, just above water level and along the foot of the wall, were rocks on which a man might stand. Perhaps from down there he could find a crack or a knothole in the wooden siding.

He let himself down carefully; the rushing water absorbed the noise he made. He had luck: just below eye level, where a board had buckled, was a crack, and by stooping a little he could see inside the mill. There were two lanterns burning, hanging from the rafters. Besides Snake and Ed there were two or three other men standing around, conversing in obscure voices above the sound of the water. But none of these was Carp. Then the sheriff saw him, removed from the others, seated on a keg with his body propped at an awkward tilt against a boiler. He never stirred. Out of the shadows around him he looked with a wan dismal glare straight ahead at some point on the wall. As the sheriff watched, he was conscious that one of the men was speaking to Carp and that Carp did not even notice; at least he did

not in any way respond. The man who had spoken to him
turned abruptly away, and the light of the lantern close to
his seamed and swarthy face exposed a look of vexation.
The sheriff received a small shock. The man was Oscar
Krantz, who worked at the hardware store not three hundred feet from the jail. The sheriff felt something distantly
alarming in this recognition, but the feeling did not last long.
He was watching Carp again.

The men stopped talking. Then the sheriff saw the figure
descending the ladder from the trap door overhead—the
deliberate movements of Flint. When he reached the floor
and turned, with a certain ponderousness, his gaze ignored
the men standing there and the greeting of a voice or two; it
quickly scanned the cluttered room and picked out Carp and
settled. But Carp did not respond, any more than he had to
Krantz. At length Flint turned to the other men and began
to talk, first to Krantz, then to an undersized, towheaded
man. His voice, with now and then an audible word emerging above the rush of water, rose and fell. In the way he
gestured with his hands there was something massive and
final, that allowed of no question, that compelled from the
men those emphatic nods of agreement. From all the men
except Ed and Snake, who seemed to move not even an
eyelash. Except Carp also. The sheriff observed that he was
not looking at the wall any more, he was looking at Flint,
at Flint's back, and the dismal glare of his eyes appeared to
have given way to something far more intense. The sheriff
found himself wishing that Flint would wheel and catch him
with that look on his face.

Flint moved then and the others followed, to the sheriff's
left and out of his field of vision. The sheriff heard voices still,
followed by other muffled sounds, but these did not long divert
his attention from Carp, who had not moved. When again he
did take note it was too late. The boat was sliding out of the

millrace, its whole length, with the upright torsos of three men, out in the moonlight now. The sheriff could only stand there hugging the wall. There was an interval of silence, a hiatus in which the boat drifted and he could feel the startled eyes of the men. With relief he saw that he was mistaken: oars appeared, the oarlocks creaked, and the boat moved off down the moonlit lake. Only then did he take in how large it was and how large the cargo of whisky that made it sit that low in the water. Just for a second he wondered where down the lake they would land it. Then he heard a voice.

Flint's body, his back to the sheriff, just missed blocking the view of Carp's face. The face was upraised, looking at Flint with an intensity to which now was added a twisted expression that exposed the white tips of his lower teeth. Flint's voice sounded clearer, as if it had risen an octave, and yet his words were no more distinct. A sudden violent gesture of his hand silenced everything but the water; and the hand, still poised in the air, for a moment screened Carp's face. Then the sheriff saw that Carp was speaking, in a voice that made no sound at all, with lips that appeared stiffly to twist and pry the words out of his mouth—some obscene and hateful words. The sheriff, exactly as if he had clearly heard, felt a cold shrinking in his viscera. And though he had not anticipated it, what happened next might have been the act of his own hand. Flint's enormous fist seemed to explode audibly in Carp's face, leaving nothing where Carp had sat.

For moments there was no movement, no sound but water; and still the big fist waited, poised, at the end of Flint's crooked arm. Carp's face, black with blood around the mouth, appeared above the keg. Uncertainly he started to get up, leaning with his shoulder against the silver boiler as he rose. He had not quite come erect when Flint, straight from his shoulder, hit him again. There was a hollow metallic thud. The boiler held him upright for a moment, like a cadaver propped at a slight angle. His knees buckled and he sank face down in an awkward heap on the floor.

For many seconds Flint stood looking down at him. He was saying something, apparently to Carp, for the boys kept on looking with the flat dispassionate gaze of animals at the humped body on the floor. Flint reached out with his foot and gave a shove that rolled Carp clear over onto his back. Carp's head and his blackened lips moved a little, but this was all. Flint spoke some last word, still to Carp, then took a lantern from a rafter and, followed by the boys, climbed the ladder out of sight.

The sheriff waited where he was until he heard them pass through the thicket of grass and saw the glow of their lantern among the trees on the hillside. Then he walked around and entered the mill. There was still one burning lantern below. As he started down the ladder he could see Carp, on an elbow now, with head drooping and sparse lank black hair almost touching the floor.

Carp showed no consciousness of his presence, even when the sheriff stood over him and called his name. A little help, some water poured on his head, would hasten his recovery. But the sheriff found that he had no wish to help him, no more than if this were a vicious snake thawing in the sun. And so he waited, content to wait.

Carp's body stirred; his head came up. Glassy eyes fastened on the sheriff's knees, then slowly climbed to his face; there they came to focus. The sheriff saw the recognition in them and he suddenly knew that he had been dreading this. From Carp's mangled lips there came an indistinguishable word. As if in reply the sheriff said harshly, "What did he beat you up for?"

Carp stared up at him. Filmy eyes, a blunt, hateful face;

and behind it, the sheriff imagined, thoughts seething like a rotten brew.

"Why did he?" the sheriff said.

Carp made an effort then and sat up, propped on one stiffened arm. He looked up again at the sheriff, stared in a way that made the sheriff long to feel the toe of his shoe smash against the bloody mouth. "Why did he beat you up?" the sheriff repeated.

The stiff lips moved, shaping the hoarse words: "You can't figure it, huh?"

The sheriff waited.

"Goddamn fool." The filmy eyes never wavered. "You mean you ain't got it figured yet?"

Between his teeth the sheriff said, "Got what figured?" and heard, in the void his question left, the ominous rushing of water. A fierce new surge of hatred was the reason that he crouched suddenly and, his face not a foot from Carp's, said as if it were venom from his mouth, "Got what figured?"

Carp faintly recoiled. Then, "Alma," he said. "Me and Alma." Carp's eyes made another startled movement, toward the trap door overhead, and then returned. "Yeah. Me and her." His virulence had come back. "It's straight now, ain't it? Me and Alma's married. Been married seven years."

The sheriff could only glare at him. Then he managed, "You're a liar."

"Liar, huh. All right. You're about to find out."

"How, find out?"

"You're just about to. You had your last of her." His voice had risen a little; he sat up straight. "You think you ever was anything to her? You wasn't nothing; she hates your guts. Nothing but something Flint put her to, to keep you muzzled. Easy done, wasn't it? You ain't got a soul to thank but Flint—he's got big plans for you. But it's all over with now."

"Unless you're lying. You mean you sat and took it? And her your wife?" Sudden hopefulness started up in the sheriff. "I think it's all lies."

A subtle change, like a pale recurrence of that first glazed expression, had come on Carp's face; the sneer was gone. "It ain't lies. Yeah, I done that; I took it. But you don't know Flint. You don't know how—"

"You mean he *made* you?"

"Yeah. In a way he did, yeah. And Alma too. You don't know what he's like. They ain't nothing or nobody but he's got them figured. And nothing he won't do."

"He did something to you, all right. Unless this is all lies."

For a moment Carp looked steadily at him. The sneer returned, giving a small twist to the crusted lips. "Yeah. Lies." He paused. "You mean to believe that, don't you? Old Flint had you figured right enough. Said you'd believe anything if it kept you from thinking you was bad. You're some good fellow all right, ain't you?"

Eye for eye the sheriff met his sneer, and felt the rekindling of his hatred.

"What went with your deputy, Mr. Sheriff?"

The sheriff tried not to waver.

"Don't know, do you?" Carp sneered. "Can't figure it. . . . You want to know?"

It seemed a great effort for the sheriff to nod his head.

"Flint killed him." Carp paused; a gleam of something like triumph stood in his eyes. "I reckon that's a lie too, though, ain't it?" Still he waited, meeting with that gleam in his eyes the sheriff's numb and heavy stare. Then he moved; with an arm braced on the silver boiler he struggled up onto his feet. But neither this effort nor his labored breathing had extinguished the light in his eyes. "Come on," he said, between breaths. "I'll show you."

It seemed a long time before these words took any final shape inside the sheriff's head. Then Carp again, saying: "Don't you want to see him, Mr. Sheriff?" He was standing upright now, clearly waiting.

There was nothing for the sheriff to do, despite the enormous effort that seemed involved, except stand up. Only then did Carp remove his gaze, turning toward the ladder and up toward the black trap door in the ceiling. He moved with still uncertain balance, bumping against a barrel as he passed, then with a movement like a lunge seizing a rung of the ladder. Abruptly he stopped, his head back. "Where'd Flint go?"

Out of a dry throat the sheriff said, "Back toward the house." He had not moved.

Carp turned his head to look back at him. "Come on, Mr. Sheriff."

With a sort of dull fascination the sheriff followed him up the ladder and into the darkness overhead. It was not so very dark, he found, once he stood upright on the floor; it seemed to be a woodenness of his legs and not the debris which, a few steps on, made him stumble. He was even slow to notice that Carp, in the doorway, had stopped again, and he came close to bumping against him. "What's the matter?" the sheriff vaguely mumbled, but the words never did take audible shape.

Carp stood there for some time, not unsteadily now; the slight occasional movements of his head were as sharp as a bird's. There was nothing to see out there. In the open space the moon defined every stem of weed and sapling, and even under the big oak tree the shadow clouded vision only a little. There came the throttled note of a screech owl somewhere close; the level sound of the water was all besides.

Then the creaking of the steps. In full moonlight, slowly, Carp descended. Again the sheriff followed without a word.

It seemed that he noticed both things in the same instant. Just in front of him Carp froze, and to his left, against the trunk of the oak tree, rising up as if from out of the ground, was the figure of a man. He knew it was Flint. Next he was conscious of Carp taking a backward step and again, though now uncertainly, halting. For a moment—because of the way he inclined first to one side, then the other—it seemed that Carp was losing his balance. If so, he recovered and once more stood as motionless as though charmed by the slow, the casual figure of Flint walking toward them out of the shade of the tree. Suddenly, as Flint loomed bigger, the sheriff felt a prickling like a gust of wintry air at the back of his neck.

He heard Flint say, in a voice that even now was vaguely reassuring, "Well, Sheriff. What you doing down here?"

He addressed himself to the sheriff exactly as if he were unconscious that Carp stood there a little to his left with pale face and blackened mouth, and moonlit eyes trained on him. After a moment, just as though he had got his answer, he added, lisping, "I thought you'd went on home. Wasn't no need of it, though. You boys going someplace?"

"I came down here to talk to him," the sheriff said.

"Yeah? Well, did you?"

"Yes."

The sheriff noticed first the little start Carp gave, and only afterward that Flint had moved and now was taking from his jumper pocket a plug of tobacco and a large switch-blade knife. With his thumbnail he flicked open the bright blade. "Now you talked to him and made friends, huh? Look like you're even heading someplace together."

"Naw we wasn't." Carp's voice was altered, as if the effort of bringing it out made him croak a little. "We wasn't together. I can't help him following me out. I ain't got nothing to do with him." Each word appeared to increase his hoarseness, but he went on. "He just come in on me. I told him . . . I told him to get out." Even for a furtive glance at the sheriff he would not turn his eyes away from Flint.

Yet Flint had his head bowed. The bright blade cut into the plug of tobacco. "You looked like you was taking him someplace," he drawled. "I think you was."

Carp stood perfectly still, watching as if hypnotized by the movements of Flint's hand closing the knife and putting it, with the plug, back in his jumper pocket. Flint held the chew in the fingers of his other hand, contemplating it. "I hate to say it. I been good to you, Leo, till now. I had my suspicions about you but I put up with you—for your daddy's sake. I don't *know* about this business, so I won't say it. But I got my suspicions. Then going after that gal of mine like that. Good thing I come here, too; I recollect what you said." Suddenly he looked straight at Carp. "Where was you taking the sheriff, Leo?"

Clearly the sheriff saw Leo swallow and saw his stiff black lips begin to move. "I wasn't taking him nowhere."

"Out in the woods someplace? To get your chance at him? Like I say, I don't *know* about that last business. But a man'll kill once like you done, Leo, is liable to do it again."

"I never went to." For a moment it seemed that he would say more.

Flint, still looking squarely at him, with a big hand holding the chew of tobacco halfway to his mouth, appeared to wait patiently. There the rushing of water, the owl again.

In a voice much more subdued than he had intended, the sheriff said, "Went to what?"

'Tell him where you been, Leo. Till a few months back."

Almost inaudibly Carp said, "In the pen."

"Tell him what for."

After a moment: "Killing a fellow."

"He never went to, though," Flint drawled. "Leo, he just couldn't turn aloose of his neck, is all. Me, I ain't going to give him a chance at mine. Not no more." He paused, looked back at Carp. Suddenly Carp twitched and by that movement seemed to gather into his eyes a whiteness from the moon.

"Get out of here, Leo." There was no drawl now in Flint's voice. It made Leo blink, an effect as if the flick of his lids had wiped the moonlight out of his eyes. "And don't turn up around here no more. Go on to the house and get your stuff. The boys is there. And don't go nowhere around Alma. She don't want no more of you."

Carp's lips parted, but this was all. Then, suddenly, the sheriff felt a small current of joy flowing in his breast.

"And don't waste no time," Flint said.

There was a moment of pause, like a suspension. Without a word Carp turned and walked away along the thicket of grass to the other end and vanished. There were rustling sounds for a moment, then nothing. There was nothing now left of that joy which the sheriff had felt a moment ago.

"All he had to do was behave hisself," Flint said. "I been good to him. Knowed his daddy. I should of run him away from here before now."

The sheriff looked bleakly at him. "Why?"

"All them things I said. Alma, for one. I ought to done it soon as he started getting hot for her. He went for her today, when we wasn't there. Tried to take it off of her. Couldn't: she was too tough. Bruised her up a little bit, though." At last, thoughtfully, he put the chew of tobacco into his mouth.

The sheriff suddenly said, "You two tell different stories."

"Huh?" Flint's speech was a little slurred now. "Yeah, I bet we do. What'd he say?"

"That she's his wife."

"Wife, huh?" Flint gazed straight ahead, his mouth faintly working, sucking at the cud in his cheek. "He'd say that. His sneaking way of shaming you off from here—if he couldn't do nothing else. He say how come she's let you court her—and him right there, standing for it?"

"Because of you. Making them."

"Yeah. Me. Had them hog-tied. I ain't run him off any too soon. . . . He figure you'd believe that?"

For all the force of his doubts the sheriff did not want to speak the words on his tongue. But if Flint was the creature which these acts made him, what bond was there to break? What bond was there between them anyway? "It didn't sound like a lie. None of it did." Then, quickly, he added, "Except just now, with you. Because he was scared." He broke off with the feeling that he had laid everything desolate.

Flint did not reply. He looked into the sheriff's face for a moment, his eyes obscure in the shadow beneath the bony ledge of his brow. Then he leaned over away from the sheriff and with scarcely a noise spat the chew of tobacco out of his mouth. "That makes me a dirty lying rascal from top to bottom, don't it?" he said in a slow neutral voice. "And a fool besides."

The sheriff found himself rejecting an impulse to deny these things, to smooth it all away.

"What else did you find out about me?"

The sheriff had to make his eyes meet Flint's. "He said you killed Hunnicutt. My deputy."

It was the sheriff's eyes that faltered. For many seconds longer Flint went on looking squarely into his face. "He said that, huh?"

"Yes," the sheriff murmured.

"That where he was taking you? To show him to you?"

The sheriff let his silence do for answer.

"And you was fixing to believe him? That I done it?"

Hesitating a moment, in a low voice the sheriff said, "Yes. I guess so. . . . If he wasn't telling the truth, why did she hide from me like that? That's what he said: that it was all over between her and me, that both of them had a belly-full of me. And other things. You needed me to—"

"Now hold on, Sheriff. I tried to tell you before. She done like that because of him jumping her that-a-way. She was mighty shook up; he even marked up her face some. I never knowed that till after you left tonight, or I'd paid him off before." He paused and looked searchingly into the sheriff's face. "You don't believe me, though, do you? Nothing I say." He paused again. "Would you believe her now? Shorely she wouldn't lie to you now, if Leo's telling the truth. Go on to the house and ask her."

In the interval that had fallen the screech owl cried. Through all the tangled confusion of questions in the sheriff's mind this cry somehow sounded like an utterance of perfect clarity. He tried to focus upon a question.

"Listen to me, Sheriff. I make whisky and I'm out the law. Didn't used to be, but the laws is changed: I'm outside now, all right. But that don't make me no such a brutish fellow as you've got to thinking. Any more than it does you for being out, Sheriff—both of us is, you know. If Leo knows that deputy's dead it's 'cause he killed him. And trying to lay it on me now. How come he knows right where his body's at?"

"I don't know," the sheriff barely murmured. Somehow he now felt a certain thankfulness for the confusion of his mind. Until all of a sudden one perfectly clear thought stood out of the tangle. It had a flatly depressing effect, so much so that it was an effort to say, "How could he have done it—by himself? And got back here that early?"

"I can't say about that. . . . But the rest of us works all day at the plant. He's the only one was here." Flint was quiet, ruminating for a second. "I been thinking about it myself. Even put it to him, like I said. But I ain't *saying* he done it, for I don't know." He let another silence fall. "If he knows where the body's at, though, then he done it. But he could of made that up."

This raised in the sheriff a faint surge of hope. For maybe, then, none of them had done it. "But he was going to take me there."

"Maybe so. But it could of been a trick, too, to get you out and off your guard. He had it in for you, Sheriff. He might of got you, too."

The sheriff knew it was only because he was suddenly very tired, but he felt almost content with this. He did not even put a stop to the little vignette that ran in his mind's eye: an encircling arm like a steel band clamping ever tighter upon his windpipe; the bitter labor of heart and lungs in his breast; and then release into a blessed dusk of crystal light, adrift, sinking from heat to coolness in the beckoning dark below.

"You needn't to worry about him no more, though, Sheriff," the kindly voice said quietly. "You go talk to Alma. You'll believe her, won't you? They ain't nothing changed. He won't bother you no more."

The sheriff was looking away, gazing out on the moonlit water and the voice seemed gently to flow across his consciousness. He had the shadowy expectation of a hand about to be laid on his shoulder. "All right," he said.

"Just give him time to get gone. I'll go on first and see he is."

"All right," the sheriff said, assenting to the voice.

Then Flint was walking away in the moonlight. When he

vanished, the sound of his passage was like a whispering in the grass. Then silence, the rush of water.

The sheriff thought of sitting down, but despite his exhaustion he never did. And when at last he started walking he knew he had no intention of going now to see Alma. He would go home, and sleep—and think tomorrow. He pushed his way through the grass and headed back up the hollow.

He had reached a point maybe halfway to the road when it came upon him that someone was following. He was certain of it until he turned around; then there was nothing to see but the moon-distorted trunks of trees down the hollow. Could it be Carp, hoping to take him from behind? This idea, though he made a sort of grasp at it, merely skipped through the sheriff's mind. There was something else: "He won't bother you no more, Sheriff." And then, "They ain't nothing changed." The sheriff found that unconsciously he had begun to walk faster, that over and over he kept repeating these last words with his tongue, and that in his mind's eye he was tensely holding his old image of Alma. As he climbed the slope to the highway at the head of the hollow he was walking fast enough to set his lungs heaving.

IX

To be certain of sleep that night he sought out tablets that his wife had left in the medicine chest. He may have taken more than he should. In any case his sleep had a quality of unnatural weightiness, like being stunned. Or maybe "put under" would better describe it, for a little eyelet of his consciousness seemed to keep watch in the general dark. And the impression he retained when at last he opened his eyes was that all night long something indistinct had been stalking him.

At first he thought that the hour was daybreak. Then he saw that the low arch of clouds was what made the light gray, that it might be any hour, and with an effort he got out of bed. It was nearly eleven o'clock, he saw by his watch on the chest of drawers. This alarmed him and sent him hurrying into the bathroom. There, the image of his face confronting him in the mirror somehow sharpened his alarm. He bent suddenly and, from the streaming faucet, laved his face as if he hoped that water might work a change in it. But the difference was only that afterward the vaguely bloated look of flesh which sagged beneath cheekbones and jaw appeared but more clearly defined by the sheen of moisture. Then he imagined that his face would not bear scrutiny—not even Pollard's. This fancy was gone in a moment, but it left him with the decision not to go to the office now. Still clad only in his shorts, shivering a little in the chill air, he descended the steps to the telephone in the hall.

He was sick, he told Pollard, then wondered about the meaning of the pause that ensued. Was Pollard smirking, as he had yesterday? It made no difference. If he felt better, the sheriff added, he would come in the afternoon.

"That revenue man called you again."

"Bascomb?" With a new kind of alarm he remembered that he should have responded before now.

"Yeah. I told him I reckoned you was up at Gatesboro."

"He didn't say what he wanted?"

"Nope. That's all."

As quickly as Pollard got off the line the sheriff called the motel where Bascomb was staying. There was no answer from Bascomb's room, and no message. The sheriff put the receiver down slowly and, with his hand yet lying on it, stood shivering from the cold on his bare skin.

He did not know what about the letter lying propped in the letter box on the door had so violently seized his attention. Not until he reached for it and saw his name in clumsy pencil scrawl and no stamp on the envelope. It trembled in his hand; he was some moments about getting his nail under the tightly sealed flap of the envelope. He held the letter up to the window light before he even tried to read it.

Deer Hank
I am sorry I ran off from you last nite and hid. I done it because of Leo Carp jumping me like he done, I was mitey shook up when you come. He even marked my face up some. Pa says he tole you some lies that ain't true. You are the only one I love and ever wood let lay a hand on me or marry. Leo is gone so he wont bother you no more or me. Come and see me tonight, I promise it wont be like last nite.

                              Your sweethart Alma

He read twice more through the still-trembling letter before its substance took real shape in his mind. The word "marry" drew his eye, transfixed it now. And then his name. He knew now that she never had called him by name before, and it was just as if he could hear the soft amorous voice speaking it in the silent house, speaking above the whisper of blood suddenly pulsing in all his veins. But there was something more. It was like an echo, increasing to an intensity that silenced his name, stilled his blood. He read again, ". . . he wont bother you no more. . . ." That echo he heard—was it not Flint's voice in the letter? Was it not all, every line of it, Flint's? With sudden agony, pausing phrase by phrase to listen, he read again through the letter. He could not be sure, could he? How could he when his emotions so distorted memory . . . ? Except for this one utterance—"he wont bother you no more"—which now had begun to repeat itself in his mind. Suddenly, "Leo is gone," the letter said.

Gone? The stillness around him in the house was like a stillness underground, a place for echoes. What was it that all night long had seemed to stalk him even in those black depths of his sleep? Like a hidden eye. Or maybe a dim pursuing voice. Could there be such things in death? No, death would be far deeper and blacker than any eye or echoing voice could ever penetrate.

A truck with gears grinding went past the house. His hand with the letter had fallen to his side; another letter, he noticed, was in the box. He saw without moving that it was from his wife and he turned his eyes away. Not quickly enough. Her railing voice, comfort and pain fused together. Sibyl's voice. He thought about her. He thought of her hair on the pillow. He thought of her warm hand swallowed up in his enormous hairy fist and then withdrawn, and then the cooling of his empty palm. Withdrawn? Had it not been he

himself who had let go of her small hand? Pain like a dull
blade probing made him turn and restlessly pace through
the house.

Into the kitchen. There was a place set at the table in
front of the window: Dora had been in that morning. Doubt-
less she had called him, with no results. But it gave him a
curious satisfaction to think how impenetrable had been the
sleep which could so perfectly seal him away from even
Dora's raucous voice. If only it had not been for that something which had stalked him through his sleep, which even
now kept stalking him like a question poised for utterance.
Abruptly he opened the oven door. It was warm inside, but
his breakfast there on the white china looked too dry and
sterile to eat. He did fix himself a cup of coffee and drank it
hot and black. But he stood while he drank it. Afterward, on
bare cold feet, he wandered aimlessly through the house
thinking, holding tight to the thought that she would be
waiting for him to come tonight. "I promise it wont be like
last nite." With this in his mind he went back to his bed at
last and tried to soothe himself into sleep again.

And he must have slept some. In any case he was all at
once awake to the feeling that he must show up at the
office soon. He began to dress himself, hurriedly at first, then
more and more deliberately. But no, he would go on. It did
matter, for tonight would not last forever.

A low grumbling of thunder reached him as he drew the
front door open. With his hand on the screen he stopped.
Past the mimosa tree where his walkway met the sidewalk a
woman, looking tentative and forlorn in the gray cloud light,
stood gazing at him. There was something so humble and
shamefaced in the way she looked at him that he thought
she was just before turning to hurry away down the street.
She did not. First she seemed about to speak; then she
started toward him, still tentative, eyes averted downward,

high brown-leather shoes that made a scuffing noise on the pavement. Then he knew who she was, must be; it was too late to evade her.

"They told me you was home, Sheriff," she said, halting at a respectful distance. "I didn't like to bother you, though, if you was sick." Their pale-blue melted quality made her eyes seem not to look directly at anything.

The sheriff managed only a nod. Already his silence had started to confound her: she stirred a little, stupidly blinking, still and forever the cringing subject of Hunnicutt's tyranny. But she did say finally, as if by straining, "I just wanted to talk to you so much . . . for just a minute."

"All right."

She blinked again, looking him not quite in the face. He opened the screen door and held it while she entered.

He did not turn on a light in the living room and the dimness half obscured the drab details of her person. She stood uncertainly before the sofa until a gesture of his hand reassured her; then she lowered herself tensely onto the cushions. There she sat upright, rigid, with vague hands folded on her lap and pale face and fringe of hair almost dissolving into the gray twilight. He remained standing, lightly propped against the bookcase, and waited numbly for her to speak. It was a long, uneasy pause, yet he could not bring himself to help her with her silent groping.

All at once she said, "He's dead, ain't he?"

"We don't know that for certain." Then he was grateful for dusk in the room.

She waited a moment. "Ain't he bound to be, though? It's been six days. What else could have gone with him?"

He tried to think what, but there was not anything. "I don't know."

"I kept on having hope . . . till yesterday. But I've give it up now. Ain't that the best thing, Sheriff? To give it up? 'Cause there ain't any hope left?"

He swallowed. "Maybe we ought to wait . . . a little longer." He had quit looking at her.

"It's just it's so hard. Not to know for sure, like with your eyes. Like to have a funeral and bury a person and know it's all done with—all but the getting over it. A person can kind of stand it then. But this-a-way. . . ." She hushed.

She was waiting for him to speak, but just then he could not bring himself even to look at her.

"Little Ralph keeps asking for him. I don't hardly know what to tell him."

He did look at her then, from the corner of his eye. "Little Ralph?"

"You know. Our little boy Ralph. You seen him. He's nine now. He come along late when we thought we wasn't never going to have no young 'un. Ralph was right proud of him."

"Yes," the sheriff murmured. He must have known this before. But now, suddenly fleshed out, it was vaguely alarming. ". . . right proud of him." He peered through the twilight, seeking again those indelible, those comforting marks of Hunnicutt's tyranny upon her. He could not see them: she was almost featureless in the gloom, only a woman's figure seated there. What he could see, in his mind, was the image of her husband's obscene, low-cunning, and vindictive face. And yet—"Ralph was right proud of him." Then there must have been another face beneath? His feeling of alarm did not pass off.

"Who could have done such a wicked thing, Sheriff—if they did?"

The sheriff felt his heart beating. But now his alarm had a different cause, a feeling that he did not know what he was about to say. He chose his words with care: "We don't know. He had been an officer a long time—long enough to make a lot of enemies. You always get some people hating you. It could have been one of them . . . maybe." Then, because of a wretchedness that abruptly had fallen upon his spirit, he added another "Maybe." A feeble and meaningless addition: shame gave another wrench to his misery.

In that moment he had moved restlessly away from the bookcase, and she, taking this for a hint, got up from the sofa. "I'll run on now. I'm sorry to bothered you, you being sick. I just felt like I had to talk to you." She was already moving toward the hall and, despite an impulse, he did not stop her.

"Of course. It's perfectly all right," he said, following her, still in the grip of his wretchedness. Could he not make definite for her at least this one small thing? Instead, with a now acute consciousness that he lied, he said, "If we come on anything definite we'll let you know right away."

"I thank you."

This time he let his impulse check a further hypocrisy on his tongue. She pushed the screen door open, and then he thought, with a swift movement, to hold it for her. The cloud light outside made her appear only a shade less drab than had the dusk of his living room. She looked back, not directly at his face, and said, "My Ralph was a good man." Her voice carried a note of insistence that somehow opened yet another depth for his misery. His reply was a nod.

He stood for a long time in the hall behind the shut front door. At length, mechanically, he took his wife's letter from the box there, opened it, and glanced at the contents. It said that she had seen Fred Herron, that he would be around in the next day or two. And that was all. The sheriff dropped the letter back into the box. By and by he tried to think where his hat was, gave it up, and walked slowly out of the house.

Outside his office door he composed himself, tried to arrange the expression of his face.

"Feeling better?" Pollard said from his seat on the window-ledge across the office.

"Yes." The sheriff sat down at his desk. He noted after a moment that Pollard's intentness had a baffling twinkle of humor. When he did comprehend it—Pollard was thinking of where he supposed the sheriff to have been last night—he made no response; he set about shuffling papers on his desk, keeping his face directed away from Pollard.

After a while, "Ever get in touch with that revenue man?" Pollard said.

"No." Still not looking up he added, "No answer at his room." The sheriff's uneasiness on this count had returned now, but it was not long before his thoughts veered back to Pollard again. The gathering silence seemed to indicate a new intentness on Pollard's part, intentness without a twinkle any more. The sheriff was thinking of how his own face had looked in the mirror, his sagging flesh with its hint of bloated-ness. Was Pollard observing this? Still the sheriff did not glance up. At last, since he could not keep on this way, he said, "Go ahead and take off. You've been on more than your share this week."

"Aw, I don't mind," Pollard said, stretching a leg.

"Shanks'll be on at six anyway. Just go ahead," the sheriff said with a curtness he had not intended. It made Pollard look at him with surprise and say, "Okay," and pick his hat from the rack. Then he was gone.

Not having anyone there to look at his face, however, made things no better for the sheriff. He watched the slow sweep of the second-hand around and around the dial of the wall clock. What about his face, what did it show? No more, at least, than did these blank and desolate faces of "wanted" men posted there on the bulletin board. How would his own look, front and profile, among them? For Hunnicutt was dead, and now maybe also . . . The sheriff gave a violent shake of his head. But what was the use of this? There was no way finally to shake reality out of his mind. He was of that gallery on his own bulletin board.

He resisted an impulse to shake his head again. Through a minute or two he sat without moving, for the thought was one that seemed to require a space of immobility before it could take root. It was true; here he was. Flint's man. All those lies to himself—contemptible rags he had gone on clutching so that he would not have to look at himself naked. All that elaborate search for Hunnicutt designed, in spite of his certain knowledge, more to distract his own than other people's eyes. Ducking and hiding from himself as if this would keep intact a picture that had ceased to describe him . . . how long ago? This question stuck. Yes, a long time, many years; he did not know when. Was not this what Hazel had perceived, that the picture was somehow a fraud?

A withering sense of humiliation brought him, finally, out of his chair. He paced to the far window, gazed emptily at the street, and paced back. He found himself stopped in front of the bulletin board at last, scrutinizing one after another the faces posted there. It was true. After a space he realized that he had spoken out loud. He spoke again, for he had found that to hear his voice affirming it was somehow a comfort to him. He began to be aware of a curious lifting of spirit and after that his thoughts were running ahead to nightfall. It would not be as in the past. Now, with the veil stripped from between them, face to face with her, it would be as it never had been before. Desire set the blood tingling in all his body.

"Hey, Sheriff."

The sheriff spun around with a violence that had to be

obvious. But Bascomb, coming through the door, made no show of noticing. "Tried to get you early this morning."

Bascomb stopped just over the threshold, and the sheriff, to give himself a moment, mumbled some words about his wife and Gatesboro. He noticed something: Bascomb's boots and khaki clothing; and also, on his pock-marked cheeks, a new flush of color. "Did you need me for something?" the sheriff said.

"Well, thought we might. It worked out all right, though. We found it."

"Found it?" The sheriff felt his lips grow stiff.

"Yes. An old mill down on the lake. Out off the Gatesboro road. Back up where a creek comes in, Cane Creek. It's the one, all right. A real whopper."

The sheriff held back for an instant. "Did you catch them?" he said, too harshly.

But Bascomb showed nothing amiss. "No. We didn't catch them. Nobody around."

The sheriff was as conscious of his face as if it were a raw wound exposed. "Do you have any idea who?"

"Maybe. I expect that McCain family down the lake a little way is in it. It's not on their land, though. Do you know anything about them?"

"McCain?" He paused. But why, now, should he stick at any lie? The thought had a force that gave him sudden confidence. "I know the name. That's all."

"That's one you didn't have on the list. Or Deputy Hunnicutt didn't. My guess is, that cost him his life. He's probably buried around there someplace."

An impulse to question this died instantly in the sheriff's mind. He found he could think of nothing to say. Fortunately Bascomb appeared distracted for the moment: he was digging in his pocket for something he could not find. It would be his key chain, was now the sheriff's one clear thought.

Bascomb gave up. "I got McCain's name from an old man down at Finch—Brock. He used to be court clerk here. He remembered McCain was convicted of moonshining eight or ten years ago. We found the mill down a hollow about a mile from his house. Dancer's Mill, it used to be. You ever know of it?"

"Yes." The sheriff paused. "I didn't know it was still standing." Another pause and: "There's no way down there any more."

"Except by water. I expect that's how they move most of the stuff. We're going to lay for them tonight. They're going to be hard to nail if we can't catch them there—nothing much to put it on them with. I hope nobody saw us today."

A sudden rumble of thunder helped the sheriff through the moment that followed. Bascomb turned to look out the door; some drops of rain had begun to fall. "I thought you'd want to know. I thought maybe you'd want to come along if you can." He looked back at the sheriff's face again and something attentive came into his eyes.

This may have been because the sheriff's confusion showed itself. But he quickly mastered it. Eye for eye he said, "When?"

"Soon as it gets dark." Bascomb glanced behind him again out into the slow sprinkling rain. "Won't be more than an hour, raining like it is."

The sheriff tightened his grip on himself. "How bad do you need me?"

"Aw, we could use you. There's eight of us, though, if you can't."

"I've got something important at seven. I can give you one of my deputies. I can come a little later myself."

"Oh, never mind," Bascomb said. "We're all right."

"I'll come a little later," the sheriff said, uneasy again.

"Well, don't mess us up, now."

"I won't. I know the way down there. I'll be careful."

"Okay," Bascomb said. "But I look for them early anyway." He gave a little good-by flip of his hand as he turned and went out, and the screen door slapped behind him.

From the door the sheriff watched him cross the street through drizzling rain and watched him disappear among trees up the courthouse lawn. He was conscious of pain in the hand with which he was gripping the door jamb. There was no question in his mind now. He turned quickly for a look at the clock; already it was well past five-thirty. By now they should be almost home, and he, if he waited for Shanks to come on at six, might not get there in time to warn them. He scrawled a note to Shanks, some lie about a call. On the steps he paused to search with his eyes among the trees on the courthouse lawn. Forcing a show of casualness he walked to the car and drove away.

X

FOR CAUTION'S SAKE the sheriff drove slowly and took a circuitous route that brought him onto the highway beyond the outskirts of town. Then he drove fast. Already the daylight was waning, horizons beginning to dissolve in the faint mist of rain; and to the southwest vivid lightning flickered under the low cloud arch. In the whole ten miles he passed no one and saw no car behind him, and this was what he had hoped for. Yet, almost, he could have wished it otherwise; there was something wrong about it. And neither the anxious speed with which he drove nor the darting evasions of his mind could quite keep off the thought that he no longer had even a voice in his destination.

At dusk he pulled up in front of the house, beside the battered car. Of course there was no one outside to greet him. What fatuous expectation was this? And was this why he required a moment to draw a long breath and then another before he got out of the car? Until he did get out he had not noticed, lying over the field and the turreted roof of the house, the dull, opaque, and colorless refulgence that was twilight or maybe the moon filtered through the clouds. Again came the shuddering of lightning, like silent cannon above the southwest horizon.

"Sheriff? That you?"

He had not heard Flint open the door, but he could see

him standing framed there, stooped with peering out into the gloom, one hand on the jamb. So the sheriff had arrived in time. Flint called again. The sheriff did not answer, but now he approached the steps. A few more paces and he was climbing, lifting one foot and then the other; and Flint, out on the porch to greet him now, said in his most cordial voice, "Sheriff, glad you come early. Wish you'd come in time for supper; we just got done. They's plenty more left over, though. Plenty."

The expression now visible in mellow lamplight from the door softened, all but obliterated, the bony rudeness of Flint's face. And then a hand—expected, the sheriff thought vaguely—fell upon the sheriff's shoulder. The warmth that rose in him unbidden, like an impulse, quite displaced the words he had been shaping. He allowed the pressure of Flint's hand and cordial voice to carry him in silence through the door, into the lighted room. But then the hand was withdrawn and he, while Flint shut the door behind him, stood feeling the moment drain like blood from his heart.

Still he did not speak. Ed, a match between his bared white teeth, sat reclining, embracing one knee, on the sofa; and Snake stood loosely propped against the wall. Snake nodded at him: he noticed this. He also noticed that there were the two of them only. For Carp was gone. But this thought merely hung in abeyance, obscured by the thing that now, at last, he must say. What if he did not say it?

Flint, still talking, had walked past and turned back to face him. "Come on over and set down. Sure you don't want some supper?"

The sheriff mumbled a negative.

"Ain't something wrong, is they, Sheriff? You're looking a little peaked."

"I'm all right." He did not go on. Maybe they did not intend to go to the mill tonight.

"Hunh. Well," Flint said. After a second he turned his face a little toward the kitchen door and called, "Hey, Alma, he's out here. Told you he'd come back." He had a little grin on his lips. "She'll be out in a second. Come on. Set down." He gestured in the direction of the sofa. "Get your foot off there, Ed."

Ed put his foot on the floor and the sheriff, without really thinking what he did, walked across to the sofa. In fact he was about to sit down—until his eyes fell on Alma. She was standing in the shadowy kitchen door with, it seemed, the suggestion of a smile upon her face. There was a moment in which he did not so much hear as feel some irrelevant nerve in his brain recording a far-off growl of thunder. Then, desire beyond any he ever had known, as fierce as an eruption, surged through all his body. For some long or short interval it held him where he stood, staring at her, seeking in the shadows there the soft details of her hair and lips and body. Then he saw, with still a further impulse of desire, that her look was summoning him. He heard a chuckle. Then:

"You ain't getting bashful in your old age, are you, Sheriff?"

Again the distant thunder. He would not tell them.

"You want to come on back?" It was her voice—like hearing it in a passionate dream.

"Yes," he answered faintly and saw her turn with a summoning gesture and vanish into the kitchen.

"That's right, Sheriff. Go on in there with her. Me and the boys got to get along anyhow. Be raining here pretty quick."

The sheriff stared straight ahead at the door where she had vanished. "Let's go, boys," he heard, and heard their movements and the sound of their shoes on the floor. If he told them . . . ? But what if he did not? Flint's voice again: "Leave you two to yourselves now. Stay long as you want,

Sheriff. You're welcome." Again the footsteps and the creak of the front door opening.

"Flint."

The footsteps ceased. He did not turn his head. After a moment Flint's voice: "Something wrong, Sheriff?"

"You can't go down there. They found it."

There was deep stillness, then thunder not so far away, and then Flint: "Huh?"

"The revenue people found it. They're laying for you down there."

He heard a step, on creaking shoes, and then another. He turned his head. The boys remained by the door, staring, but Flint had moved closer and stopped near the lamp. It was a changed face, with rigid jaw dropped down and narrowed eyes and brutal spurs and ridges of bone detailed beneath the skin. "How do you know?"

"The head agent, Bascomb, told me. This evening. He wanted me to come along."

Flint did not move.

"I didn't want to tell you," the sheriff said. "Then you started to leave."

"How'd they find it?" There was no unction in his voice now.

"Got your name from an old man at Gatesboro, that used to be court clerk. He told him you had been caught before. They lucked up on the mill."

Flint made a slight abortive gesture with his hand, left it in a fist. Then, with a jolt, the sheriff's eye fell on Alma in the kitchen door. It was toward her that he said, almost blurting it out, "They can't get you, though; it's not on your land. They can't pin it on you, no matter what they think. They'd have to catch you and they can't now. Because you know." His voice had taken on an unpleasant, a begging note, which he did not even try to purge. "All you've got to

do is lie low for a while. Then you can start up again somewhere else. I know places. I've seen—"

"You know you ain't made no mistake?" Flint broke in. He
seemed not to have been listening to this last.

The sheriff, as if he had run suddenly out of breath, could
only shake his head.

Flint watched him for a moment longer. Then he wheeled
around toward the boys with a motion so violent that both
of them flinched; Snake's elbow thumped against the door.
But nothing followed. Flint's fist, though tightly clenched,
hung at his side, but for a space he did not move or utter
any sound. There was thunder again, quite near, making
vibrations in the house. Flint walked across the room and
stood as though examining a shattered place in the wall
plaster. "How come you didn't stop them?" he said harshly,
then turned around quickly to glare at the sheriff.

"How could I? I didn't even know about it," he heard himself answer. There was another pause. "But I can help you—"

"You was a help, wasn't you, Sheriff? . . . Yeah. Sheriff."
His voice was an ugly rasping sneer. "I ought to known the
likes of you—God damn you. I ought to known. . . ." His voice,
declining, spent itself in a string of hoarse and broken obscen-
ities. Then, almost a shout, "I had it going. By God I had
it—" Violently he wheeled and drove his fist straight and
hard into the wall. There was a rending and then a crash of
fallen plaster. Moments later a fragment as large as a plate
detached itself from the ceiling and struck the floor and
scattered around his feet.

Flint drew his fist carefully out of the wall. It appeared
mangled, vivid with blood, and he stood regarding it as if
lost in astonished meditation upon the fact. From the door
the boys looked on with the flat inanimate gaze of dummies
stationed there. But there *was* movement in the room.

The sheriff turned his head in time to see her nearly at the top of the stairs, already vanishing into the darkness above. She passed out of sight. He waited for sounds of her passage across the landing overhead, but for all his intensity he heard nothing. This fact, at last, wakened desperate hope in him. He began to see at the top of the steps shadows take shape against the darkness and gesture to him with shadow arms. They were not real. There were footsteps. But these were behind him, were Flint's, were the sound of his pacing across the room.

The sheriff saw him reach the kitchen door and stop and stand there with his big head down. The bloody fist appeared, then vanished, cupped in his other hand. There came a flash, then a stroke of thunder, but Flint did not stir. At length it was the sheriff who moved, half a step toward Flint, and said—or rather, blurted, for he knew how foolish was this waste of breath—"Look. If you'd listen to me. I'm with you now, I'm in it too. I know—"

A sound like a hawking up of phlegm issued from Flint's throat. "Get out of my sight. You ain't even fit to . . ." He had turned with ferocious abruptness toward the sheriff, but then, as if the movement had purged his fury, his eyes seemed to register nothing where the sheriff stood. In a moment he started walking, a very slow, deliberate walk that brought him nearly close enough to brush against the sheriff as he passed and crossed the room toward the open bedroom door. There he stopped again.

The stillness, without sound of thunder now, was like an element holding the sheriff locked fast in his tracks. And the longer he submitted to it, the more he felt himself unmanned. He was straining his ears, but there was no sound from overhead. The thing was there to do. Finally he began it, with a step that shattered the silence of the room and drew all eyes but Flint's upon him. Once on the stairs he did not care about the eyes that followed, like guns trained, until he had climbed out of sight.

Her door was open, her room in light from the burning lamp on the table beside her bed. He was conscious how the pulse beat at his temples as he crossed the landing and stepped through her door. She was seated on the unmade bed, hands on her bare knees, looking squarely at him. A dizzying uprush of desire in him for the moment caused her to appear quite pale and unsubstantial. Then her voice:

"What do you want?"

It was harsh, flat; it jolted him. Only after seconds did the rude irony of it surface in his brain.

"You don't really reckon you're going to get any more off of me, do you?" The bitter mockery was evident, but there was no hint of it in her face. This was hard and blank, with rude graven jaw—Flint's jaw. Flint's very self, in woman's body. But still the heat in his blood did not die out.

"Do you?" After a second she gave what maybe was a laugh, a tiny eruption of laughter, that did bring a change in her face. He mumbled something. The change was in her eyes, a squint that seemed to gather the pupils in fine diamond points. He knew he had seen it before. And what he saw—what she now meant that he should see—clearly and simply was hate.

His little added shock of bewilderment for a moment prevented his noticing the display of mocking triumph in her movements. She leaned back and, resting upon an elbow, one foot drawn up onto the bed, exposed above the hem of her skirt the length of a bare white thigh. And yet he stared at it. Until she said:

"You know, I ain't sorry they found it. I couldn't of stood for you no longer."

For the first time he noticed the marks on her cheek and

forehead. Something slipped into place. "Then Flint gave you those bruises?"

"You think it was Leo? You reckon I'd of took it from Leo? He wasn't much better than you."

Hesitating, "Then he isn't your husband?" he uncertainly said.

"Didn't he tell you he was?"

It seemed to be the greedy malice of her gaze that kept him from shaking off his bewilderment. "Is it the truth?"

"Sure it is. Anybody but you would of believed him. I been married to Leo a long time." When the sheriff said nothing, she added, "It ain't like it's Leo beat you out, though. I had enough of him too—long time ago."

After a space, though the question just now seemed irrelevant, he said, "Where is Leo?"

"How do I know?"

But the question and the answer both had receded already in his mind, and he was saying, "It was Flint all the time, then—making you."

"He never had to make me—not till the last. I done it for him willing. He ain't like you. Or none of you. He's a man; he don't have to lie to hisself. But you're *good*, ain't you, Sheriff? Sheriff!" she repeated, with a small venomous gust of laughter. "That's when I commenced getting good and sick— when I seen that. Flint, he seen it right off."

The sheriff stood mute. All of what had been his desire now seemed to lie like weight against his heart. His silence must have goaded her.

"You know what he said you was like?" She paused just long enough for a quick answer. "He said you was like a no-account guard dog, that didn't need a thing but a little feeding up and petting in the dark. That's all you are. You ain't nothing."

It was the astonishing bitterness of these words, bringing

her upright on the bed again, that jarred him out of his stupor. But not into clarity: now it was rage that mastered him. A broken obscene oath burst from his lips and two lunging strides brought him near enough to deliver the blow he already had aimed. It struck her high on the head, hard enough to knock her sideways and send her tumbling from the bed. The lamp teetered, fell with a crash, and darkness came down like another blow.

For an interval he could neither hear nor see anything in the room, and it was precisely as if that stroke of his fist had exploded a nightmare. He stood panting. From somewhere outside of the house a voice reached him. Then a tremulous flare of lightning revealed her stark face against the bedside, looking up at him, and he knew that all his rage toward her was spent. Everything was spent. There was darkness again, and low muttering thunder.

"You dirty bastard."

Her hoarse whisper in the dark did not so much as take him by surprise; for a second he held the notion that he had heard it only within his mind. He knew it would come again.

"You ain't nothing. That make you feel like a man, hitting me? You're a brave one, ain't you?"

"No," he murmured.

"Try that out on Flint and see what you are." Her voice, already receding, grew still beneath a crescendo of thunder. There was a hush once more, but he still waited, listening for the voice.

"Go on. Try it on Flint—he's the one to blame. See if you can stand up to him." She paused, and he heard her draw breath. Then harshly: "You lying bastard, you couldn't stand up to nothing."

After a space he asked, "You really don't know where Carp is?"

"I don't know nothing about him."

"And Hunnicutt?"

This time she hesitated. A surface of his mind recorded the sound of an engine starting up. With renewed scorn she said, "What do you want to know for? You been getting along fine. It don't bother you long as you don't know—it don't hurt your conscience."

"I know. Flint killed him," he murmured.

"If he did, you're in it too. Don't forget that . . . Sheriff."

He did not answer. In another flash of lightning her cold face emerged for a second.

"If you really got to know, go ask Flint. *Make* him tell you."

For a long moment more he stood there. "All right," he said, and turned deliberately and left the room.

One simple thing was in his mind: that he would stand face to face with Flint. Between them now was only a moment, a flight of stairs upon which he had already set foot. A few steps more, however, and he came to a halt, in confusion. The room below was empty. For some seconds he felt that he could not get his mind or his body either in motion again. What set him moving at last, down the stairs and across the room to the open front door, was the memory of having heard somewhere a car engine start up. Outside he descended the steps in darkness that blinded him. Lightning flared; the empty field stood in his eyes. Where his, where both the cars had been, there was nothing.

Recurrent lightning kept confirming this until it became a fact for him. Yet he took some steps across the yard and stopped where his car had been parked. Gone where? They would have to come back. And then . . . What did he have in mind to do? Or was there anything at all he could do now—except look at it? Rather, look at himself. His brave resolve of this afternoon, his fatuous expectations. And now

this, blasting him loose from the last of those childish lies
that he had hugged so hard to his breast. ". . . a little feeding up and petting in the dark. That's all you are. You ain't
nothing." Her voice in all its envenomed clarity came back as
if he were hearing it again, hearing her call it out from the
house, from up in the turret where the colored panes threw
tinted light on her twisted face. Like grace, he ironically
thought, remembering from long ago light through the
stained church window falling upon him. Very long ago,
another world—a world fit only for children. There was
nothing left of it. One violent shake of his head sent it
spinning out of his memory and he stood looking where now
and then in ghastly spasms of lightning an empty meadow
flared out of the dark. What was there left of him, without
any lies?

A drop of rain touched his forehead. Just after this, as if
this had put vision back into his eyes, he saw a light. It
was far out across the field; at first he thought that it was a
will-o'-the-wisp floating close to the ground. Another moment
convinced him that it was a lantern which someone was
carrying. It was moving away from him, toward the woods,
toward the mill. Seconds afterward lightning rent the dark
and he saw, sketched against a blackness of trees, the
diminished figure of a man. It was not much more than a
glimpse and the distance was considerable; for assurance he
had only the violent quickening of his pulse. Yet this seemed
to be enough. He delayed maybe the space of a few heartbeats before he started, walking neither fast nor slow, past
the house, the outbuildings, with rain in his face now and
eyes tensely fastened upon the distant lantern-glow.

The lantern began to flicker off and on. It vanished
entirely, then reappeared as a vague aura of scattered shifting light. Then he could not see it at all; he had only the
intermittent flashes of lightning, making the timber loom, by

which to fix his gaze on the point where the lantern had vanished. Except when it blurred his eyes he did not notice the rain coursing in streams down his face and neck. Here was the edge of the woods. He was conscious of altered sound, the hiss of rain among the foliage, and of the denser night that gathered around him. Lightning showed the path just steps to his right.

At length, passing among the stark trunks of beech trees in scattered columns, he saw the lantern-light again. It was not in front of him any longer, but off on his left, drifting like a mist among the trees. Heading toward it, he quit the path.

His progress brought him no closer; the light kept moving, drawing him on through wet leafy branches and vines that slid or scraped without pain across his face, through brush and creepers that snared his feet. Yet, because of the hissing rain and the loam and wet leaves underfoot, his passage made no noise at all, no more than did the aura of light distantly floating on through the timber.

The light disappeared and then he was walking blind. But soon he saw it again, below him, down an incline. He halted. For one thing the light had stopped moving, and for another it was much closer to him now. With caution he advanced down the slope and presently stopped again. For now he saw not merely the glow but the flame of the lantern flashing on and off behind the moving legs of the man who carried it. But the man was not going anywhere. He seemed to be pacing back and forth, slowly, with here and there an extended pause. One pause lasted longer than the others. At the end of it he lifted the lantern and turned the wick up until the flame illuminated from head to foot the big stooped body of Flint. Then Flint set the lantern on the ground.

The circle of ground in rainy lantern-light, under the low,

dense foliage of a beech, was a nearly flat place like a ter-
race in the slope. Flint walked almost out of the light, and
there, a hulking shadow half-fused with the tree trunk,
crouched down. Above the hiss of rain there was a dim
clashing noise. He came into the light again with his arms
full of wet dead leaves and, pausing close to the lantern,
began to sprinkle them over the ground at his feet. Already
the sheriff knew what it meant. Still he kept watching, held
in a kind of numb absorption, while Flint with all the deliberation of a celebrant gathered more leaves in the darkness
and repeated the action and yet another time repeated it. At
last he stood at a little distance from the lantern, his body
stooped, his eyes dark hollows under the dripping hat brim,
and peered around at his handiwork.

Flint did not seem satisfied; turning his head he scanned
the dark around him. Until suddenly he stopped, with his
eyes trained directly toward the sheriff. But no, Flint had
not seen him, for after taking a few steps forward he bent
and picked up a large dead limb and turned with it back
toward the lantern. It seemed no choice of the sheriff's that
he took this moment in which to step forward down the
slope.

"Who's that?" Flint had violently wheeled around. But
after this he waited in silence, a hand in his jumper pocket,
watching the sheriff advance into the light. When the sheriff
had come to a stop, Flint said, "What you doing here,
Sheriff?"

Flint stood in front of the lantern and the glow, tracing
the lines of his hulking form, seemed to give him dimen-
sions larger than life. It was impossible to see his eyes. The
sheriff felt no response from the violence he tried to summon
up; he let his gaze fall away to the limb that lay over the
scattered leaves. "I followed you."

"Yeah. I figured that. What'd you do it for?"

Still that violence would not come. In a low voice he said, "It doesn't matter. This is the place, isn't it? Where you buried him."

Seconds later his eye was attracted by the glint of water drops that had begun to fall from the brim of Flint's hat. Then he saw the shadowy lips part, say, "He would of told on us, Sheriff."

The sheriff felt something like a small click inside his brain, but this was all. With a heaviness no greater than before he said, "Then that's Carp there."

Maybe Flint blinked; nothing else.

"Is Hunnicutt there too?"

"They ain't nobody there, Sheriff."

"Is he there?"

"Naw, I told you. You ain't seen nobody, have you?"

The rain fell, hissing, dripping with little glints of light from the hat brim over the shadowy face. "I'm not playing that game any more."

"Not, huh?" Flint paused. "Yes you are too, Sheriff. You wanted to play, and you're in. You're in up to your neck. . . . And no use to blame me. Ain't got nobody to blame but yourself."

"I'm quitting now." He said this with a sharp little thrill in his blood, as of mingled dread and exaltation. And a second later, almost fiercely, he added, "I want to know if Hunnicutt's there too."

"All right, Sheriff. Yeah, he's there. Both of them's there. But that ain't nothing to you. Naw, you ain't quitting. They ain't a way in the world for you to get out."

The sheriff saw, not for the first time, that Flint's hand was in his jumper pocket. But that thrill in the sheriff's blood seemed only the keener for this. "I'm already out, Flint."

For a space he imagined that he could see Flint's eyes

emerging from the shadows. "Naw," Flint said at last. "You're in. For good." His tone loosened just a bit as he added, "The boys'll be back with your car pretty soon—soon as they get rid of the other'n. You go on home. Get you some sleep. You keep your mouth shut, won't nothing happen."

The sheriff gave time for the voice to die entirely out of his head. "I'm going to turn us in, Flint."

There was no response; there was rain.

"I'm not blaming you—for me. I did that."

Then the sheriff was certain that he could see Flint's eyes glaring from the deep black sockets underneath the brutal ledge of bone. But Flint did not move.

There were only three or four paces between them. It was not fear but only a perfectly calculating prudence that caused the sheriff to toy with the idea of taking several steps backward before he turned around. Yet already he knew that he would not do this: he would simply turn and walk away. What was he waiting for? His feet might have had root in the wet loam, and his blood, instead of throbbing, seemed to trill like sound along his veins. Then, in one deliberate movement, he turned away.

But instantly, before even a noise reached him, he saw Flint's shadow heave. He wheeled in time to glimpse the flash of steel and to strike out hard with his hand. He hit Flint's arm, deflecting it sideways, so that the blade slashed empty air. But the tree limb was somehow at his feet and, trying to wheel back around, he stumbled. The blade felt most like a hot spark flashing in between his ribs behind; it was inside that the blow seemed to land. The effect was in his eyes, like smoke, and then like blazing light. Then came rage. He was conscious of all his strength contracted and then expelled in one violent upward surge of his elbow. It struck hard—a dull wooden sound. He had to blink several times before he could see, and then he was not sure whether this swaying motion was his own or that of Flint down on hands and knees with drooping head.

He was aware of feeling compassion for Flint; there came a temptation to kneel down and help him, to lift his head, to hold him upright. But sudden pain in the sheriff's chest brought a certain clarity. He must be quick. The lantern was close by. He thought to kick it as he passed, bringing the darkness down, and the rain. He headed downhill.

He kept stumbling, colliding with trees in the dark and with bushes that ripped at his garments and his flesh. Increasingly it grew hard to breathe; the air seemed not enough and the little there was seemed to burn his lungs. He had a raging thirst. Then he could no longer remember where he was headed with such blind precipitate haste. Was Flint pursuing him? He stepped into water and instantly sank down.

Lying with chin and chest in the cold water he sucked it until his belly would not hold any more. It was not enough, the fire was still there, but his clarity had returned. Lifting his head in a flicker of lightning he saw the lake. It was the mill he was headed for; this was the branch in the hollow and there to his right the hillside he must climb. Pain flashed beneath his ribs when he moved. He lay still and thought of the lake, its surface flecked with rain, and thought of his feverish body floating or drifting in limpid coolness downward toward the dark. Again the lightning. He stood up with a violence that yielded nothing to his pain.

He was crawling by the time he reached the crest of the slope. But he got to his feet once more and stumbled on. A vision of the mill and Bascomb there came and went in his mind, even though he kept forgetting what was so urgent in this. And in between these visions the scene would shift. Even the rain would stop and he would be walking through familiar woods, barefoot, in the moist air of a twilight thick with scent of pollen. Not far ahead was where the ridge broke in a sharp decline. At the foot was a creek with a log bridge to cross, and beyond this the fragrance of a blooming orchard in back of the house.

And sure enough, at last, the ground began to decline, grew steep. But something was wrong; he became confused, for there was no path down the hill. He stopped, holding to a tree on the steep embankment, hazily trying to get things straight. The lake and then the mill flashed out of the dark below him. This was where he was headed; there was no orchard. But the water was just below him, he must bear to his right, and the bank was steep. The effort seemed too much; he held to the tree, leaning against it with his head. But did he not now hear something besides the hiss of rain— footsteps, Flint coming down on him? Yet it was not fear of Flint that made him let go of the tree: his one firm thought was that this time at least he must not be thwarted. He took a step and reached out for the next shadowy tree trunk, and missed. The bank beneath him started to sway. He cried out. The earth reeled and struck the whole length of his body a blow that made the lightning flare, and then another that extinguished everything.

He was floating in cool water, held afloat by a last desperate effort of his hand that he knew could not be maintained much longer. He wanted to let go. Yet he held on still, and when he felt his hand begin to slip he strained out of his body what he knew to be the last thing he had left, a cry. Or did he get it out? Every bodily sense seemed blasted by the fierce stroke of his pain. Except his vision. Was it only pain that now had produced this blinding brilliance in his eyes? And the something warm that had closed tight upon his wrist, his hand. He felt his body shifting, in tow, and then the back of his head plowing the slick mud bank.

He was very cold, except for his hand. He faintly under-
stood that this was because he still had not let go of the
warm hand that had towed him from the water. Now he
tried to clutch it tighter, and could not. Though much dim-
mer than before, there was light in his eyes again. And then
a voice as from a distance, "By God, it's Sheriff Tawes."

He did understand the words, but it was the voice, sounding with a strange human sweetness, that sank deep and
maintained itself like a kind of radiance in his mind. Even
when everything in the world had ceased to exist for him,
this radiance still lived on for a little while.